# TEACHER'S PET PUBLICATIONS

PUZZLE PACK
for
A Christmas Carol
based on the book by
Charles Dickens

Written by
William T. Collins

INTRODUCTION

If you already own the LitPlan for this title, this Puzzle Pack will refresh your Unit Resource Materials and Vocabulary Resource Materials sections plus give you additional materials you can substitute into the tests. If you do not already have a complete LitPlan, these pages will give you some supplemental materials to use with your own plan. There are two main groups of materials: one set for unit words (such as characters' names, symbols, places, etc.) and one set for vocabulary words associated with the book.

WORD LIST

There is a word list for both the unit words and the vocabulary words. These lists show you which words are being used in the materials and the clues or definitions being used for those words. You may want to give students a word list with clues/definitions to help them, or you may want students to only have a word list (without clues/definitions) if you want them to work a little harder. Both are available for duplication. The word lists can also be your "calling key" for the bingo games.

FILL IN THE BLANK AND MATCHING

There are 4 each of the fill in the blank and matching worksheets for both the unit and vocabulary words. These pages can be used either as extra worksheets for students or as objective parts of a unit test. They can be done individually if students need extra help or as a whole class activity to review the material covered.

MAGIC SQUARES

The magic squares not only reinforce the material covered but also work on reasoning and math skills. Many teachers have told us that their students really enjoy doing these!

WORD SEARCH PUZZLES

The word search words go in all directions, as indicated on your answer keys. Two of the word search puzzles have the clues listed rather than the words. This makes the puzzle a little more difficult, but it reinforces the material better. Two word search puzzles have words only for students who find the clue puzzles too difficult.

CROSSWORD PUZZLES

Both unit and vocabulary word sections have 4 crossword puzzles.

BINGO CARDS

There are 32 individual bingo cards for the unit words and 32 individual bingo cards for the vocabulary words. You can use your word list as a "call list," calling the words at random and marking them off of your list as you go, or you could use the flash cards by cutting them apart and drawing the words at random from a hat (or box or whatever). To make a better review, you might ask for the definition and spelling of each word as you call it out–or you could call out the definitions and have students tell you the words they need to look for on the puzzle.

JUGGLE LETTERS

The vocabulary juggle letter game is intended to help students learn the spellings of the words. One sheet has the definitions listed on it as an extra help for students who need it or to reinforce the definitions if you choose to do so.

FLASH CARDS

We've included a set of vocabulary flash cards you can duplicate, cut, and fold for your students. Some teachers make a few sets for general use by the class; others make a set for each student. Some teachers duplicate them for each student and have the students cut & fold their own. You can cut out just the words and put them in a hat, have each student pick out one word and write the definition and a sentence for that word. Students then swap words and papers, with the next student adding a sentence of his own under the last one. You can have students swap as many times as you like. Each time the student will read the sentences written prior to his own and then add a sentence. You can cut out the words and definitions separately and play "I Have; Who Has?" Each student in the room draws a word and definition. The first student says, "I have (the name of the word). Who has the definition?" The student with the definition reads it then says, "I have (the name of the vocabulary word she has). Who has the definition?" The round continues until all words and definitions have been given.

Christmas Carol Word List

No.	Word	Clue/Definition
1.	BELLE	Scrooge's former fiancee
2.	BLACK	Garment color of Spirit of Christmas Yet To Come
3.	CRATCHIT	Scrooge's clerk Bob
4.	CHAINS	Marley was wearing the ones he forged in life
5.	DICKENS	Author
6.	CHARWOMAN	Took Scrooge's bed curtains
7.	CHRISTMAS	Scrooge did not miss it
8.	EVE	When Marley appeared: Christmas ___
9.	SCUTTLE	Scrooge told Bob to buy a new coal ___
10.	DOOM	Written on the boy's brow
11.	KNOCKER	It turned into Marley's face
12.	EBENEZER	Scrooge's first name
13.	CAP	Worn by first Spirit: extinguisher ___
14.	FAN	Scrooge's sister
15.	FEZZIWIG	Scrooge's former master
16.	FRED	Scrooge's nephew
17.	INVITATION	Good afternoon was Scrooge's reply to his nephew's ___
18.	GRAVE	Last spirit showed Scrooge his name on a ___ stone
19.	GREEN	Robe color of Spirit of Christmas Present
20.	HUMBUG	Scrooge's expression
21.	IGNORANCE	The boy under the spirit's robe
22.	JACOB	Marley's first name
23.	JOE	Old man looking at Scrooge's things
24.	LAUNDRESS	Mrs. Dilber's job
25.	LONDON	Setting of novel
26.	MARLEY	Dead partner
27.	MARTHA	Cratchit's daughter
28.	DILBER	Laundress who took Scrooge's things
29.	NEPHEW	Invited Scrooge to Christmas dinner
30.	SCRATCH	Nickname for the dead businessman: Old ___
31.	PAST	White hair; face without wrinkles
32.	PETER	Cratchit's older son, looking for a job
33.	PRESENT	Said Tiny Tim might die
34.	RECLAMATION	What first spirit came for
35.	SCROOGE	Covetous old sinner
36.	TAVERN	Where Scrooge ate
37.	TIM	Cratchit's lame youngest son: Tiny ___
38.	TOPPER	Pretended to be blind during the game
39.	TURKEY	Scrooge sent it to the Cratchit home
40.	UNDERTAKER	Took Scrooge's seal, pencil case, sleeve-buttons, and brooch
41.	WANT	The girl under the spirit's robe
42.	WAREHOUSE	Scrooge's place of business
43.	WHITE	Tunic color of the Spirit of Christmas Past

_____   1. Written on the boy's brow

_____   2. Tunic color of the Spirit of Christmas Past

_____   3. The girl under the spirit's robe

_____   4. Scrooge told Bob to buy a new coal ___

_____   5. Author

_____   6. What first spirit came for

_____   7. Scrooge's former fiancee

_____   8. Took Scrooge's seal, pencil case, sleeve-buttons, and brooch

_____   9. It turned into Marley's face

_____   10. Robe color of Spirit of Christmas Present

_____   11. Took Scrooge's bed curtains

_____   12. The boy under the spirit's robe

_____   13. Scrooge's sister

_____   14. Cratchit's older son, looking for a job

_____   15. Scrooge did not miss it

_____   16. Old man looking at Scrooge's things

_____   17. Setting of novel

_____   18. Nickname for the dead businessman: Old ___

_____   19. Cratchit's lame youngest son: Tiny ___

_____   20. Invited Scrooge to Christmas dinner

DOOM	1. Written on the boy's brow
WHITE	2. Tunic color of the Spirit of Christmas Past
WANT	3. The girl under the spirit's robe
SCUTTLE	4. Scrooge told Bob to buy a new coal ___
DICKENS	5. Author
RECLAMATION	6. What first spirit came for
BELLE	7. Scrooge's former fiancee
UNDERTAKER	8. Took Scrooge's seal, pencil case, sleeve-buttons, and brooch
KNOCKER	9. It turned into Marley's face
GREEN	10. Robe color of Spirit of Christmas Present
CHARWOMAN	11. Took Scrooge's bed curtains
IGNORANCE	12. The boy under the spirit's robe
FAN	13. Scrooge's sister
PETER	14. Cratchit's older son, looking for a job
CHRISTMAS	15. Scrooge did not miss it
JOE	16. Old man looking at Scrooge's things
LONDON	17. Setting of novel
SCRATCH	18. Nickname for the dead businessman: Old ___
TIM	19. Cratchit's lame youngest son: Tiny ___
NEPHEW	20. Invited Scrooge to Christmas dinner

_____   1. Robe color of Spirit of Christmas Present

_____   2. Laundress who took Scrooge's things

_____   3. Took Scrooge's bed curtains

_____   4. Scrooge's expression

_____   5. When Marley appeared: Christmas ___

_____   6. Scrooge's sister

_____   7. Scrooge did not miss it

_____   8. Scrooge's nephew

_____   9. Cratchit's older son, looking for a job

_____ 10. Scrooge's former fiancee

_____ 11. Dead partner

_____ 12. Tunic color of the Spirit of Christmas Past

_____ 13. It turned into Marley's face

_____ 14. Nickname for the dead businessman: Old ___

_____ 15. Marley was wearing the ones he forged in life

_____ 16. Marley's first name

_____ 17. Last spirit showed Scrooge his name on a ___ stone

_____ 18. Cratchit's daughter

_____ 19. Scrooge sent it to the Cratchit home

_____ 20. Written on the boy's brow

GREEN	1. Robe color of Spirit of Christmas Present
DILBER	2. Laundress who took Scrooge's things
CHARWOMAN	3. Took Scrooge's bed curtains
HUMBUG	4. Scrooge's expression
EVE	5. When Marley appeared: Christmas ___
FAN	6. Scrooge's sister
CHRISTMAS	7. Scrooge did not miss it
FRED	8. Scrooge's nephew
PETER	9. Cratchit's older son, looking for a job
BELLE	10. Scrooge's former fiancee
MARLEY	11. Dead partner
WHITE	12. Tunic color of the Spirit of Christmas Past
KNOCKER	13. It turned into Marley's face
SCRATCH	14. Nickname for the dead businessman: Old ___
CHAINS	15. Marley was wearing the ones he forged in life
JACOB	16. Marley's first name
GRAVE	17. Last spirit showed Scrooge his name on a ___ stone
MARTHA	18. Cratchit's daughter
TURKEY	19. Scrooge sent it to the Cratchit home
DOOM	20. Written on the boy's brow

_____ 1. Scrooge's former fiancee

_____ 2. Scrooge's clerk Bob

_____ 3. Where Scrooge ate

_____ 4. Garment color of Spirit of Christmas Yet To Come

_____ 5. Said Tiny Tim might die

_____ 6. Scrooge sent it to the Cratchit home

_____ 7. When Marley appeared: Christmas ___

_____ 8. Took Scrooge's seal, pencil case, sleeve-buttons, and brooch

_____ 9. Scrooge's sister

_____ 10. What first spirit came for

_____ 11. Scrooge's nephew

_____ 12. Scrooge's place of business

_____ 13. Pretended to be blind during the game

_____ 14. Tunic color of the Spirit of Christmas Past

_____ 15. The boy under the spirit's robe

_____ 16. Mrs. Dilber's job

_____ 17. Marley was wearing the ones he forged in life

_____ 18. White hair; face without wrinkles

_____ 19. Good afternoon was Scrooge's reply to his nephew's ___

_____ 20. Dead partner

A Christmas Carol Fill In The Blank 3 Answer Key

BELLE	1. Scrooge's former fiancee
CRATCHIT	2. Scrooge's clerk Bob
TAVERN	3. Where Scrooge ate
BLACK	4. Garment color of Spirit of Christmas Yet To Come
PRESENT	5. Said Tiny Tim might die
TURKEY	6. Scrooge sent it to the Cratchit home
EVE	7. When Marley appeared: Christmas ___
UNDERTAKER	8. Took Scrooge's seal, pencil case, sleeve-buttons, and brooch
FAN	9. Scrooge's sister
RECLAMATION	10. What first spirit came for
FRED	11. Scrooge's nephew
WAREHOUSE	12. Scrooge's place of business
TOPPER	13. Pretended to be blind during the game
WHITE	14. Tunic color of the Spirit of Christmas Past
IGNORANCE	15. The boy under the spirit's robe
LAUNDRESS	16. Mrs. Dilber's job
CHAINS	17. Marley was wearing the ones he forged in life
PAST	18. White hair; face without wrinkles
INVITATION	19. Good afternoon was Scrooge's reply to his nephew's ___
MARLEY	20. Dead partner

_____   1. Cratchit's older son, looking for a job

_____   2. Scrooge's sister

_____   3. Scrooge sent it to the Cratchit home

_____   4. Nickname for the dead businessman: Old ___

_____   5. Cratchit's daughter

_____   6. Scrooge's clerk Bob

_____   7. Old man looking at Scrooge's things

_____   8. Robe color of Spirit of Christmas Present

_____   9. Tunic color of the Spirit of Christmas Past

_____   10. Cratchit's lame youngest son: Tiny ___

_____   11. Scrooge's expression

_____   12. White hair; face without wrinkles

_____   13. Good afternoon was Scrooge's reply to his nephew's ___

_____   14. The boy under the spirit's robe

_____   15. Scrooge's former master

_____   16. It turned into Marley's face

_____   17. Marley was wearing the ones he forged in life

_____   18. Garment color of Spirit of Christmas Yet To Come

_____   19. Worn by first Spirit: extinguisher ___

_____   20. Invited Scrooge to Christmas dinner

PETER	1. Cratchit's older son, looking for a job
FAN	2. Scrooge's sister
TURKEY	3. Scrooge sent it to the Cratchit home
SCRATCH	4. Nickname for the dead businessman: Old ___
MARTHA	5. Cratchit's daughter
CRATCHIT	6. Scrooge's clerk Bob
JOE	7. Old man looking at Scrooge's things
GREEN	8. Robe color of Spirit of Christmas Present
WHITE	9. Tunic color of the Spirit of Christmas Past
TIM	10. Cratchit's lame youngest son: Tiny ___
HUMBUG	11. Scrooge's expression
PAST	12. White hair; face without wrinkles
INVITATION	13. Good afternoon was Scrooge's reply to his nephew's ___
IGNORANCE	14. The boy under the spirit's robe
FEZZIWIG	15. Scrooge's former master
KNOCKER	16. It turned into Marley's face
CHAINS	17. Marley was wearing the ones he forged in life
BLACK	18. Garment color of Spirit of Christmas Yet To Come
CAP	19. Worn by first Spirit: extinguisher ___
NEPHEW	20. Invited Scrooge to Christmas dinner

A Christmas Carol Matching 1

___ 1. EBENEZER   A. Covetous old sinner

___ 2. SCROOGE   B. Scrooge's place of business

___ 3. FRED   C. The girl under the spirit's robe

___ 4. TIM   D. Cratchit's lame youngest son: Tiny ___

___ 5. WANT   E. Took Scrooge's seal, pencil case, sleeve-buttons, and brooch

___ 6. LONDON   F. Dead partner

___ 7. CHAINS   G. Scrooge's sister

___ 8. TOPPER   H. Scrooge's nephew

___ 9. MARTHA   I. Where Scrooge ate

___10. UNDERTAKER   J. Mrs. Dilber's job

___11. CHRISTMAS   K. Nickname for the dead businessman: Old ___

___12. TAVERN   L. Garment color of Spirit of Christmas Yet To Come

___13. DILBER   M. Setting of novel

___14. CHARWOMAN   N. Marley's first name

___15. EVE   O. Took Scrooge's bed curtains

___16. BELLE   P. Scrooge's former fiancee

___17. PRESENT   Q. Pretended to be blind during the game

___18. FAN   R. Scrooge's first name

___19. SCRATCH   S. Worn by first Spirit: extinguisher ___

___20. BLACK   T. Cratchit's daughter

___21. MARLEY   U. Laundress who took Scrooge's things

___22. LAUNDRESS   V. Said Tiny Tim might die

___23. CAP   W. Scrooge did not miss it

___24. WAREHOUSE   X. When Marley appeared: Christmas ___

___25. JACOB   Y. Marley was wearing the ones he forged in life

A Christmas Carol Matching 1 Answer Key

R - 1. EBENEZER   A. Covetous old sinner

A - 2. SCROOGE   B. Scrooge's place of business

H - 3. FRED   C. The girl under the spirit's robe

D - 4. TIM   D. Cratchit's lame youngest son: Tiny ___

C - 5. WANT   E. Took Scrooge's seal, pencil case, sleeve-buttons, and brooch

M - 6. LONDON   F. Dead partner

Y - 7. CHAINS   G. Scrooge's sister

Q - 8. TOPPER   H. Scrooge's nephew

T - 9. MARTHA   I. Where Scrooge ate

E -10. UNDERTAKER   J. Mrs. Dilber's job

W -11. CHRISTMAS   K. Nickname for the dead businessman: Old ___

I - 12. TAVERN   L. Garment color of Spirit of Christmas Yet To Come

U -13. DILBER   M. Setting of novel

O -14. CHARWOMAN   N. Marley's first name

X -15. EVE   O. Took Scrooge's bed curtains

P -16. BELLE   P. Scrooge's former fiancee

V -17. PRESENT   Q. Pretended to be blind during the game

G -18. FAN   R. Scrooge's first name

K -19. SCRATCH   S. Worn by first Spirit: extinguisher ___

L -20. BLACK   T. Cratchit's daughter

F -21. MARLEY   U. Laundress who took Scrooge's things

J - 22. LAUNDRESS   V. Said Tiny Tim might die

S -23. CAP   W. Scrooge did not miss it

B -24. WAREHOUSE   X. When Marley appeared: Christmas ___

N -25. JACOB   Y. Marley was wearing the ones he forged in life

A Christmas Carol Matching 2

___ 1. TOPPER   A. Good afternoon was Scrooge's reply to his nephew's ___

___ 2. DILBER   B. Marley was wearing the ones he forged in life

___ 3. FAN   C. Tunic color of the Spirit of Christmas Past

___ 4. WHITE   D. Garment color of Spirit of Christmas Yet To Come

___ 5. EVE   E. Mrs. Dilber's job

___ 6. MARLEY   F. Where Scrooge ate

___ 7. SCRATCH   G. Dead partner

___ 8. CHAINS   H. Pretended to be blind during the game

___ 9. RECLAMATION   I. Laundress who took Scrooge's things

___10. UNDERTAKER   J. Took Scrooge's seal, pencil case, sleeve-buttons, and brooch

___11. DICKENS   K. Scrooge's sister

___12. INVITATION   L. Setting of novel

___13. CHRISTMAS   M. The boy under the spirit's robe

___14. TAVERN   N. Scrooge's former master

___15. FEZZIWIG   O. What first spirit came for

___16. BLACK   P. Cratchit's older son, looking for a job

___17. LONDON   Q. Scrooge sent it to the Cratchit home

___18. MARTHA   R. Cratchit's daughter

___19. PRESENT   S. Old man looking at Scrooge's things

___20. PETER   T. When Marley appeared: Christmas ___

___21. IGNORANCE   U. Nickname for the dead businessman: Old ___

___22. TURKEY   V. White hair; face without wrinkles

___23. JOE   W. Said Tiny Tim might die

___24. PAST   X. Author

___25. LAUNDRESS   Y. Scrooge did not miss it

A Christmas Carol Matching 2 Answer Key

H - 1. TOPPER   A. Good afternoon was Scrooge's reply to his nephew's ___

I - 2. DILBER   B. Marley was wearing the ones he forged in life

K - 3. FAN   C. Tunic color of the Spirit of Christmas Past

C - 4. WHITE   D. Garment color of Spirit of Christmas Yet To Come

T - 5. EVE   E. Mrs. Dilber's job

G - 6. MARLEY   F. Where Scrooge ate

U - 7. SCRATCH   G. Dead partner

B - 8. CHAINS   H. Pretended to be blind during the game

O - 9. RECLAMATION   I. Laundress who took Scrooge's things

J - 10. UNDERTAKER   J. Took Scrooge's seal, pencil case, sleeve-buttons, and brooch

X - 11. DICKENS   K. Scrooge's sister

A - 12. INVITATION   L. Setting of novel

Y - 13. CHRISTMAS   M. The boy under the spirit's robe

F - 14. TAVERN   N. Scrooge's former master

N - 15. FEZZIWIG   O. What first spirit came for

D - 16. BLACK   P. Cratchit's older son, looking for a job

L - 17. LONDON   Q. Scrooge sent it to the Cratchit home

R - 18. MARTHA   R. Cratchit's daughter

W - 19. PRESENT   S. Old man looking at Scrooge's things

P - 20. PETER   T. When Marley appeared: Christmas ___

M - 21. IGNORANCE   U. Nickname for the dead businessman: Old ___

Q - 22. TURKEY   V. White hair; face without wrinkles

S - 23. JOE   W. Said Tiny Tim might die

V - 24. PAST   X. Author

E - 25. LAUNDRESS   Y. Scrooge did not miss it

A Christmas Carol Matching 3

___ 1. KNOCKER   A. Scrooge told Bob to buy a new coal ___

___ 2. CAP   B. Author

___ 3. CHAINS   C. Scrooge's expression

___ 4. TOPPER   D. Written on the boy's brow

___ 5. FRED   E. Setting of novel

___ 6. MARTHA   F. When Marley appeared: Christmas ___

___ 7. UNDERTAKER   G. Pretended to be blind during the game

___ 8. GRAVE   H. Scrooge's nephew

___ 9. PETER   I. Dead partner

___10. IGNORANCE   J. Worn by first Spirit: extinguisher ___

___11. RECLAMATION   K. Cratchit's daughter

___12. EVE   L. Took Scrooge's seal, pencil case, sleeve-buttons, and brooch

___13. TAVERN   M. Cratchit's older son, looking for a job

___14. FAN   N. Last spirit showed Scrooge his name on a ___ stone

___15. BELLE   O. Scrooge sent it to the Cratchit home

___16. LAUNDRESS   P. The boy under the spirit's robe

___17. TURKEY   Q. Mrs. Dilber's job

___18. CHARWOMAN   R. Scrooge's sister

___19. SCUTTLE   S. Marley was wearing the ones he forged in life

___20. DICKENS   T. Where Scrooge ate

___21. DOOM   U. Robe color of Spirit of Christmas Present

___22. GREEN   V. What first spirit came for

___23. LONDON   W. Scrooge's former fiancee

___24. MARLEY   X. It turned into Marley's face

___25. HUMBUG   Y. Took Scrooge's bed curtains

A Christmas Carol Matchig 3 Answer Key

X - 1. KNOCKER   A. Scrooge told Bob to buy a new coal ___

J - 2. CAP   B. Author

S - 3. CHAINS   C. Scrooge's expression

G - 4. TOPPER   D. Written on the boy's brow

H - 5. FRED   E. Setting of novel

K - 6. MARTHA   F. When Marley appeared: Christmas ___

L - 7. UNDERTAKER   G. Pretended to be blind during the game

N - 8. GRAVE   H. Scrooge's nephew

M - 9. PETER   I. Dead partner

P -10. IGNORANCE   J. Worn by first Spirit: extinguisher ___

V -11. RECLAMATION   K. Cratchit's daughter

F -12. EVE   L. Took Scrooge's seal, pencil case, sleeve-buttons, and brooch

T -13. TAVERN   M. Cratchit's older son, looking for a job

R -14. FAN   N. Last spirit showed Scrooge his name on a ___ stone

W ·15. BELLE   O. Scrooge sent it to the Cratchit home

Q -16. LAUNDRESS   P. The boy under the spirit's robe

O -17. TURKEY   Q. Mrs. Dilber's job

Y -18. CHARWOMAN   R. Scrooge's sister

A -19. SCUTTLE   S. Marley was wearing the ones he forged in life

B -20. DICKENS   T. Where Scrooge ate

D -21. DOOM   U. Robe color of Spirit of Christmas Present

U -22. GREEN   V. What first spirit came for

E -23. LONDON   W. Scrooge's former fiancee

I - 24. MARLEY   X. It turned into Marley's face

C -25. HUMBUG   Y. Took Scrooge's bed curtains

A Christmas Carol Matching 4

___ 1. PRESENT   A. Scrooge sent it to the Cratchit home

___ 2. SCRATCH   B. Took Scrooge's bed curtains

___ 3. LONDON   C. Scrooge told Bob to buy a new coal ___

___ 4. HUMBUG   D. Author

___ 5. UNDERTAKER   E. Tunic color of the Spirit of Christmas Past

___ 6. PETER   F. Covetous old sinner

___ 7. CAP   G. Scrooge's expression

___ 8. CHARWOMAN   H. Good afternoon was Scrooge's reply to his nephew's ___

___ 9. PAST   I. Pretended to be blind during the game

___10. SCROOGE   J. What first spirit came for

___11. NEPHEW   K. Garment color of Spirit of Christmas Yet To Come

___12. DOOM   L. Scrooge's clerk Bob

___13. TOPPER   M. Written on the boy's brow

___14. INVITATION   N. Said Tiny Tim might die

___15. KNOCKER   O. The girl under the spirit's robe

___16. SCUTTLE   P. Nickname for the dead businessman: Old ___

___17. CHAINS   Q. Marley was wearing the ones he forged in life

___18. BLACK   R. Took Scrooge's seal, pencil case, sleeve-buttons, and brooch

___19. TURKEY   S. Invited Scrooge to Christmas dinner

___20. TAVERN   T. Setting of novel

___21. WHITE   U. Where Scrooge ate

___22. RECLAMATION   V. It turned into Marley's face

___23. DICKENS   W. Worn by first Spirit: extinguisher ___

___24. WANT   X. Cratchit's older son, looking for a job

___25. CRATCHIT   Y. White hair; face without wrinkles

A Christmas Carol Matching 4 Answer Key

N - 1. PRESENT   A. Scrooge sent it to the Cratchit home

P - 2. SCRATCH   B. Took Scrooge's bed curtains

T - 3. LONDON   C. Scrooge told Bob to buy a new coal ___

G - 4. HUMBUG   D. Author

R - 5. UNDERTAKER   E. Tunic color of the Spirit of Christmas Past

X - 6. PETER   F. Covetous old sinner

W - 7. CAP   G. Scrooge's expression

B - 8. CHARWOMAN   H. Good afternoon was Scrooge's reply to his nephew's ___

Y - 9. PAST   I. Pretended to be blind during the game

F - 10. SCROOGE   J. What first spirit came for

S - 11. NEPHEW   K. Garment color of Spirit of Christmas Yet To Come

M - 12. DOOM   L. Scrooge's clerk Bob

I - 13. TOPPER   M. Written on the boy's brow

H - 14. INVITATION   N. Said Tiny Tim might die

V - 15. KNOCKER   O. The girl under the spirit's robe

C - 16. SCUTTLE   P. Nickname for the dead businessman: Old ___

Q - 17. CHAINS   Q. Marley was wearing the ones he forged in life

K - 18. BLACK   R. Took Scrooge's seal, pencil case, sleeve-buttons, and brooch

A - 19. TURKEY   S. Invited Scrooge to Christmas dinner

U - 20. TAVERN   T. Setting of novel

E - 21. WHITE   U. Where Scrooge ate

J - 22. RECLAMATION   V. It turned into Marley's face

D - 23. DICKENS   W. Worn by first Spirit: extinguisher ___

O - 24. WANT   X. Cratchit's older son, looking for a job

L - 25. CRATCHIT   Y. White hair; face without wrinkles

A Christmas Carol Magic Squares 1

Match the definition with the vocabulary word. Put your answers in the magic squares below. When your answers are correct, all columns and rows will add to the same number.

A. BELLE   E. HUMBUG   I. DOOM   M. EVE
B. TIM   F. WHITE   J. GRAVE   N. SCRATCH
C. CHRISTMAS G. DILBER   K. BLACK   O. RECLAMATION
D. PETER   H. INVITATION   L. LAUNDRESS   P. TOPPER

1. When Marley appeared: Christmas ___
2. Tunic color of the Spirit of Christmas Past
3. Good afternoon was Scrooge's reply to his nephew's ___
4. What first spirit came for
5. Mrs. Dilber's job
6. Scrooge did not miss it
7. Scrooge's former fiancee
8. Last spirit showed Scrooge his name on a ___ stone

9. Garment color of Spirit of Christmas Yet To Come
10. Cratchit's older son, looking for a job
11. Cratchit's lame youngest son: Tiny ___
12. Written on the boy's brow
13. Nickname for the dead businessman: Old ___
14. Scrooge's expression
15. Laundress who took Scrooge's things
16. Pretended to be blind during the game

A=	B=	C=	D=
E=	F=	G=	H=
I=	J=	K=	L=
M=	N=	O=	P=

A Christmas Carol Magc Squares 1 Answer Key

Match the definition with the vocabulary word. Put your answers in the magic squares below. When your answers are correct, all columns and rows will add to the same number.

A. BELLE
B. TIM
C. CHRISTMAS
D. PETER

E. HUMBUG
F. WHITE
G. DILBER
H. INVITATION

I. DOOM
J. GRAVE
K. BLACK
L. LAUNDRESS

M. EVE
N. SCRATCH
O. RECLAMATION
P. TOPPER

1. When Marley appeared: Christmas ___
2. Tunic color of the Spirit of Christmas Past
3. Good afternoon was Scrooge's reply to his nephew's ___
4. What first spirit came for
5. Mrs. Dilber's job
6. Scrooge did not miss it
7. Scrooge's former fiancee
8. Last spirit showed Scrooge his name on a ___ stone

9. Garment color of Spirit of Christmas Yet To Come
10. Cratchit's older son, looking for a job
11. Cratchit's lame youngest son: Tiny ___
12. Written on the boy's brow
13. Nickname for the dead businessman: Old ___
14. Scrooge's expression
15. Laundress who took Scrooge's things
16. Pretended to be blind during the game

A=7	B=11	C=6	D=10
E=14	F=2	G=15	H=3
I=12	J=8	K=9	L=5
M=1	N=13	O=4	P=16

A Christmas Carol Magic Squares 2

Match the definition with the vocabulary word. Put your answers in the magic squares below. When your answers are correct, all columns and rows will add to the same number.

A. MARLEY   E. DOOM   I. TIM   M. KNOCKER
B. PRESENT   F. PAST   J. FRED   N. NEPHEW
C. TOPPER   G. WAREHOUSE   K. EBENEZER   O. UNDERTAKER
D. INVITATION   H. CHRISTMAS   L. MARTHA   P. CAP

1. Took Scrooge's seal, pencil case, sleeve-buttons, and brooch
2. Good afternoon was Scrooge's reply to his nephew's ___
3. Scrooge's nephew
4. Written on the boy's brow
5. Cratchit's lame youngest son: Tiny ___
6. White hair; face without wrinkles
7. Worn by first Spirit: extinguisher ___
8. Pretended to be blind during the game
9. Scrooge did not miss it
10. Scrooge's first name
11. Dead partner
12. Invited Scrooge to Christmas dinner
13. Said Tiny Tim might die
14. It turned into Marley's face
15. Scrooge's place of business
16. Cratchit's daughter

A=	B=	C=	D=
E=	F=	G=	H=
I=	J=	K=	L=
M=	N=	O=	P=

A Christmas Carol Magic Squares 2 Answer Key

Match the definition with the vocabulary word. Put your answers in the magic squares below. When your answers are correct, all columns and rows will add to the same number.

A. MARLEY   E. DOOM   I. TIM   M. KNOCKER
B. PRESENT   F. PAST   J. FRED   N. NEPHEW
C. TOPPER   G. WAREHOUSE   K. EBENEZER   O. UNDERTAKER
D. INVITATION H. CHRISTMAS   L. MARTHA   P. CAP

1. Took Scrooge's seal, pencil case, sleeve-buttons, and brooch
2. Good afternoon was Scrooge's reply to his nephew's ___
3. Scrooge's nephew
4. Written on the boy's brow
5. Cratchit's lame youngest son: Tiny ___
6. White hair; face without wrinkles
7. Worn by first Spirit: extinguisher ___
8. Pretended to be blind during the game
9. Scrooge did not miss it
10. Scrooge's first name
11. Dead partner
12. Invited Scrooge to Christmas dinner
13. Said Tiny Tim might die
14. It turned into Marley's face
15. Scrooge's place of business
16. Cratchit's daughter

A=11	B=13	C=8	D=2
E=4	F=6	G=15	H=9
I=5	J=3	K=10	L=16
M=14	N=12	O=1	P=7

A Christmas Carol Magic Squares 3

Match the definition with the vocabulary word. Put your answers in the magic squares below. When your answers are correct, all columns and rows will add to the same number.

A. MARTHA   E. CHRISTMAS   I. NEPHEW   M. FEZZIWIG
B. EBENEZER   F. BELLE   J. WAREHOUSE   N. RECLAMATION
C. UNDERTAKER   G. IGNORANCE   K. TOPPER   O. TAVERN
D. LAUNDRESS   H. LONDON   L. CRATCHIT   P. KNOCKER

1. Setting of novel
2. Cratchit's daughter
3. Scrooge's first name
4. The boy under the spirit's robe
5. Scrooge's place of business
6. Where Scrooge ate
7. It turned into Marley's face
8. Invited Scrooge to Christmas dinner

9. Pretended to be blind during the game
10. What first spirit came for
11. Scrooge's former master
12. Scrooge's clerk Bob
13. Scrooge did not miss it
14. Mrs. Dilber's job
15. Took Scrooge's seal, pencil case, sleeve-buttons, and brooch
16. Scrooge's former fiancee

A=	B=	C=	D=
E=	F=	G=	H=
I=	J=	K=	L=
M=	N=	O=	P=

25

A Christmas Carol Magic Squares 3 Answer Key

Match the definition with the vocabulary word. Put your answers in the magic squares below. When your answers are correct, all columns and rows will add to the same number.

A. MARTHA   E. CHRISTMAS   I. NEPHEW   M. FEZZIWIG
B. EBENEZER   F. BELLE   J. WAREHOUSE   N. RECLAMATION
C. UNDERTAKER G. IGNORANCE   K. TOPPER   O. TAVERN
D. LAUNDRESS   H. LONDON   L. CRATCHIT   P. KNOCKER

1. Setting of novel
2. Cratchit's daughter
3. Scrooge's first name
4. The boy under the spirit's robe
5. Scrooge's place of business
6. Where Scrooge ate
7. It turned into Marley's face
8. Invited Scrooge to Christmas dinner
9. Pretended to be blind during the game
10. What first spirit came for
11. Scrooge's former master
12. Scrooge's clerk Bob
13. Scrooge did not miss it
14. Mrs. Dilber's job
15. Took Scrooge's seal, pencil case, sleeve-buttons, and brooch
16. Scrooge's former fiancee

A=2	B=3	C=15	D=14
E=13	F=16	G=4	H=1
I=8	J=5	K=9	L=12
M=11	N=10	O=6	P=7

A Christmas Carol Magic Squares 4

Match the definition with the vocabulary word. Put your answers in the magic squares below. When your answers are correct, all columns and rows will add to the same number.

A. JOE
B. TOPPER
C. PETER
D. CHAINS

E. BLACK
F. PAST
G. WHITE
H. MARLEY

I. DICKENS
J. CRATCHIT
K. PRESENT
L. BELLE

M. SCRATCH
N. EVE
O. UNDERTAKER
P. CAP

1. Dead partner
2. Nickname for the dead businessman: Old ___
3. Pretended to be blind during the game
4. Said Tiny Tim might die
5. Scrooge's clerk Bob
6. Cratchit's older son, looking for a job
7. Worn by first Spirit: extinguisher ___
8. Garment color of Spirit of Christmas Yet To Come

9. Took Scrooge's seal, pencil case, sleeve-buttons, and brooch
10. White hair; face without wrinkles
11. Author
12. Marley was wearing the ones he forged in life
13. Old man looking at Scrooge's things
14. Scrooge's former fiancee
15. Tunic color of the Spirit of Christmas Past
16. When Marley appeared: Christmas ___

A=	B=	C=	D=
E=	F=	G=	H=
I=	J=	K=	L=
M=	N=	O=	P=

A Christmas Carol Magic Squares 4 Answer Key

Match the definition with the vocabulary word. Put your answers in the magic squares below. When your answers are correct, all columns and rows will add to the same number.

A. JOE
B. TOPPER
C. PETER
D. CHAINS

E. BLACK
F. PAST
G. WHITE
H. MARLEY

I. DICKENS
J. CRATCHIT
K. PRESENT
L. BELLE

M. SCRATCH
N. EVE
O. UNDERTAKER
P. CAP

1. Dead partner
2. Nickname for the dead businessman: Old ___
3. Pretended to be blind during the game
4. Said Tiny Tim might die
5. Scrooge's clerk Bob
6. Cratchit's older son, looking for a job
7. Worn by first Spirit: extinguisher ___
8. Garment color of Spirit of Christmas Yet To Come

9. Took Scrooge's seal, pencil case, sleeve-buttons, and brooch
10. White hair; face without wrinkles
11. Author
12. Marley was wearing the ones he forged in life
13. Old man looking at Scrooge's things
14. Scrooge's former fiancee
15. Tunic color of the Spirit of Christmas Past
16. When Marley appeared: Christmas ___

A=13	B=3	C=6	D=12
E=8	F=10	G=15	H=1
I=11	J=5	K=4	L=14
M=2	N=16	O=9	P=7

A Christmas Carol Word Search 1

```
D I L B E R H U M B U G M P L O N D O N
O W Q W X X G N N K L Z J C E A B X X S
O T Z G R L X D Y H N P Z T M T S P Q J
M P U E B E N E Z E R X T O T S E C Z V
F C B R B Z R R G Z Z Z W X S C C R D C
E V J T K X Z T Y M D R R E D U F Z M T
Z K Y V B E C A B H A F R Z Z T X Q D Q
Z C C Y J T Y K J H S D C R A T C H I T
I N H F N Y F E C W N F C W P L W G D F
W Q P R W L H R M U R C D B X E X W C Q
I S R W I F C M A X G R I B M Z E M T Q
G C E N C S W L R H D E C F E H M G A H
F R S N S X T H T N K K K C P L B C V Q
L A E Z B E G M H C E C E E A W L S E G
V T N I N V I T A T I O N T O P P E R H
F C T S J E H L I S G N S N I M A E N J
M H C Y C F B H Y D L K T A T M E S X W
M A K M Y R W S T V J N W W K N C N T B
X N R I G N O R A N C E J A C O B I F J
N H X L G Q R O C L W Z B L Z J H A R C
F W L V E L N G G J J B C V B O L H E Y
G R A V E Y W A R E H O U S E E P C D J
```

Author (7)
Covetous old sinner (7)
Cratchit's daughter (6)
Cratchit's lame youngest son: Tiny ___ (3)
Cratchit's older son, looking for a job (5)
Dead partner (6)
Garment color of Spirit of Christmas Yet To Come (5)
Good afternoon was Scrooge's reply to his nephew's ___ (10)
Invited Scrooge to Christmas dinner (6)
It turned into Marley's face (7)
Last spirit showed Scrooge his name on a ___ stone (5)
Laundress who took Scrooge's things (6)
Marley was wearing the ones he forged in life (6)
Marley's first name (5)
Mrs. Dilber's job (9)
Nickname for the dead businessman: Old ___ (7)
Old man looking at Scrooge's things (3)
Pretended to be blind during the game (6)
Robe color of Spirit of Christmas Present (5)

Said Tiny Tim might die (7)
Scrooge did not miss it (9)
Scrooge sent it to the Cratchit home (6)
Scrooge told Bob to buy a new coal ___ (7)
Scrooge's clerk Bob (8)
Scrooge's expression (6)
Scrooge's first name (8)
Scrooge's former fiancee (5)
Scrooge's former master (8)
Scrooge's nephew (4)
Scrooge's place of business (9)
Scrooge's sister (3)
Setting of novel (6)
The boy under the spirit's robe (9)
The girl under the spirit's robe (4)
Took Scrooge's bed curtains (9)
Took Scrooge's seal, pencil case, sleeve-buttons, and brooch (10)
Tunic color of the Spirit of Christmas Past (5)
When Marley appeared: Christmas ___ (3)
Where Scrooge ate (6)
White hair; face without wrinkles (4)
Worn by first Spirit: extinguisher ___ (3)
Written on the boy's brow (4)

A Christmas Carol Word Search 1 Answer Key

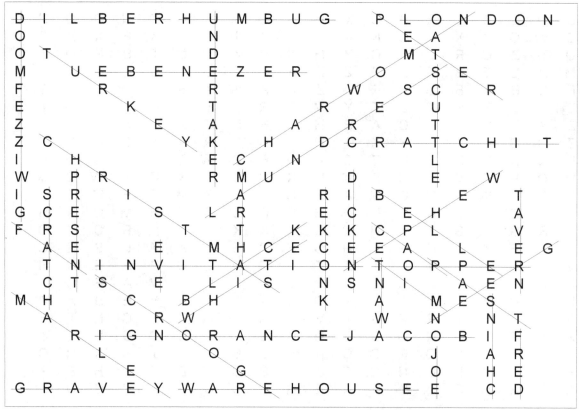

Author (7)
Covetous old sinner (7)
Cratchit's daughter (6)
Cratchit's lame youngest son: Tiny ___ (3)
Cratchit's older son, looking for a job (5)
Dead partner (6)
Garment color of Spirit of Christmas Yet To Come (5)
Good afternoon was Scrooge's reply to his nephew's ___ (10)
Invited Scrooge to Christmas dinner (6)
It turned into Marley's face (7)
Last spirit showed Scrooge his name on a ___ stone (5)
Laundress who took Scrooge's things (6)
Marley was wearing the ones he forged in life (6)
Marley's first name (5)
Mrs. Dilber's job (9)
Nickname for the dead businessman: Old ___ (7)
Old man looking at Scrooge's things (3)
Pretended to be blind during the game (6)
Robe color of Spirit of Christmas Present (5)

Said Tiny Tim might die (7)
Scrooge did not miss it (9)
Scrooge sent it to the Cratchit home (6)
Scrooge told Bob to buy a new coal ___ (7)
Scrooge's clerk Bob (8)
Scrooge's expression (6)
Scrooge's first name (8)
Scrooge's former fiancee (5)
Scrooge's former master (8)
Scrooge's nephew (4)
Scrooge's place of business (9)
Scrooge's sister (3)
Setting of novel (6)
The boy under the spirit's robe (9)
The girl under the spirit's robe (4)
Took Scrooge's bed curtains (9)
Took Scrooge's seal, pencil case, sleeve-buttons, and brooch (10)
Tunic color of the Spirit of Christmas Past (5)
When Marley appeared: Christmas ___ (3)
Where Scrooge ate (6)
White hair; face without wrinkles (4)
Worn by first Spirit: extinguisher ___ (3)
Written on the boy's brow (4)

```
M  Z  K  P  K  K  R  G  V  B  Y  D  Y  E  T  P  N  Q  M  H
D  G  J  R  J  G  R  X  H  E  J  H  E  G  I  T  D  P  P  Y
G  K  S  E  I  A  F  Z  L  L  P  M  L  O  H  V  A  N  M  Y
L  P  F  S  V  G  B  H  L  L  E  H  R  O  C  S  J  R  S  F
G  R  E  E  N  T  N  A  W  E  T  M  A  R  T  H  A  E  V  E
C  E  R  N  Z  A  A  O  M  U  E  O  M  C  A  Q  C  K  X  S
H  B  E  T  F  Z  B  V  R  N  R  G  P  S  R  S  O  C  H  H
A  L  C  K  P  C  I  K  E  A  G  V  W  P  C  M  B  O  S  L
R  I  L  W  K  Y  E  W  P  R  N  R  A  D  E  W  F  N  C  G
W  D  A  Y  C  Y  L  S  I  D  N  C  R  S  O  R  H  K  R  Y
O  L  M  D  T  R  T  G  L  G  C  B  E  S  E  O  J  I  A  M
M  M  A  Q  I  S  T  G  O  T  V  K  H  D  N  T  M  N  T  S
A  C  T  N  M  J  U  K  N  U  N  Q  O  D  G  C  R  E  C  E
N  B  I  P  H  B  C  G  D  Y  N  G  U  N  S  E  P  P  H  K
L  D  O  S  M  V  S  B  O  Z  X  D  S  N  Z  T  S  H  M  R
V  I  N  U  D  X  B  G  N  H  C  W  E  E  T  L  J  E  L  Q
R  C  H  A  I  N  S  T  W  X  T  H  N  R  B  C  M  W  E  S
K  K  J  H  B  D  P  H  T  Q  Q  E  L  D  T  F  Z  O  M  Q
L  E  M  G  L  K  F  J  Y  V  B  K  V  Z  Q  A  J  N  Q  S
M  N  R  X  A  Z  L  J  N  E  X  S  V  B  B  X  K  J  S  V
T  S  C  T  C  H  R  I  S  T  M  A  S  X  D  T  P  E  Y  L
Q  P  F  B  K  L  A  U  N  D  R  E  S  S  Q  N  W  H  R  H
```

Author (7)
Covetous old sinner (7)
Cratchit's daughter (6)
Cratchit's lame youngest son: Tiny ___ (3)
Cratchit's older son, looking for a job (5)
Dead partner (6)
Garment color of Spirit of Christmas Yet To Come (5)
Invited Scrooge to Christmas dinner (6)
It turned into Marley's face (7)
Last spirit showed Scrooge his name on a ___ stone (5)
Laundress who took Scrooge's things (6)
Marley was wearing the ones he forged in life (6)
Marley's first name (5)
Mrs. Dilber's job (9)
Nickname for the dead businessman: Old ___ (7)
Old man looking at Scrooge's things (3)
Pretended to be blind during the game (6)
Robe color of Spirit of Christmas Present (5)
Said Tiny Tim might die (7)
Scrooge did not miss it (9)

Scrooge sent it to the Cratchit home (6)
Scrooge told Bob to buy a new coal ___ (7)
Scrooge's clerk Bob (8)
Scrooge's expression (6)
Scrooge's first name (8)
Scrooge's former fiancee (5)
Scrooge's former master (8)
Scrooge's nephew (4)
Scrooge's place of business (9)
Scrooge's sister (3)
Setting of novel (6)
The boy under the spirit's robe (9)
The girl under the spirit's robe (4)
Took Scrooge's bed curtains (9)
Took Scrooge's seal, pencil case, sleeve-buttons, and brooch (10)
Tunic color of the Spirit of Christmas Past (5)
What first spirit came for (11)
When Marley appeared: Christmas ___ (3)
Where Scrooge ate (6)
White hair; face without wrinkles (4)
Worn by first Spirit: extinguisher ___ (3)
Written on the boy's brow (4)

A Christmas Carol Word Search 2 Answer Key

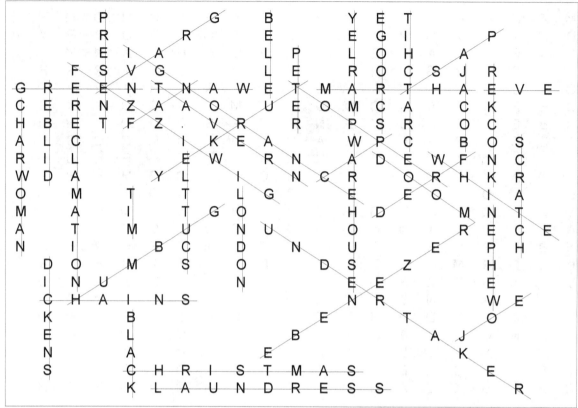

Author (7)
Covetous old sinner (7)
Cratchit's daughter (6)
Cratchit's lame youngest son: Tiny ___ (3)
Cratchit's older son, looking for a job (5)
Dead partner (6)
Garment color of Spirit of Christmas Yet To
  Come (5)
Invited Scrooge to Christmas dinner (6)
It turned into Marley's face (7)
Last spirit showed Scrooge his name on a ___
  stone (5)
Laundress who took Scrooge's things (6)
Marley was wearing the ones he forged in life
  (6)
Marley's first name (5)
Mrs. Dilber's job (9)
Nickname for the dead businessman: Old ___
  (7)
Old man looking at Scrooge's things (3)
Pretended to be blind during the game (6)
Robe color of Spirit of Christmas Present (5)
Said Tiny Tim might die (7)
Scrooge did not miss it (9)

Scrooge sent it to the Cratchit home (6)
Scrooge told Bob to buy a new coal ___ (7)
Scrooge's clerk Bob (8)
Scrooge's expression (6)
Scrooge's first name (8)
Scrooge's former fiancee (5)
Scrooge's former master (8)
Scrooge's nephew (4)
Scrooge's place of business (9)
Scrooge's sister (3)
Setting of novel (6)
The boy under the spirit's robe (9)
The girl under the spirit's robe (4)
Took Scrooge's bed curtains (9)
Took Scrooge's seal, pencil case,
  sleeve-buttons, and brooch (10)
Tunic color of the Spirit of Christmas Past (5)
What first spirit came for (11)
When Marley appeared: Christmas ___ (3)
Where Scrooge ate (6)
White hair; face without wrinkles (4)
Worn by first Spirit: extinguisher ___ (3)
Written on the boy's brow (4)

A Christmas Carol Word Search 3

```
L B K L P H Q K B L N W N T M F M Y J Q J Z M S R
H H H K Z C Z V Z P W D D R X F W X P K R D Q M W
V C R K J Q T M K C W S F X X S M Z C W H T H B J
X P R C B K T B B Q R A G T T K C C L S F Y H V R
B S F X F Y L N P V J T R D Y Z V S T P N C G W D
K J X Z W Y S G H Y T V M E Y R Z X G R D C G N C
M J W D N Z Y T S Z N S L F H X L W T E M T V H V
V V V M Q G I N G T K M W L K O A V P S R S R M W
B P X A L H Y J Q D W S S P O V U M M E N I B R V
K F E R C L T O Y V H N H G N N S S N S V Z W P
P A S T W S N E K C I D D M O O D R E T G R E E N
N H A H E Y K C V A T G I N C R R O M Q A H C G X
R R Y A B R F W H E E T N L L G E A N Y P V N O M
C E F O U C B C A Z H H B O B F S N K E S S E O R
W F C T B A E G G N U U J E R E S Q N L C C I R V
C A X L Y P I B A R T N M E L A R X O R R U N C N
J N A W A W B M E C A S D B P L N G C A A T V S Z
L C K J I M O T P N P V G E U S E C K M T T I G L
K Y V Z R W A D R Z E X E W R G Y C E R C L T R S
B B Z Y R W T T C T F Z Y Q M T P F R C H E A Y Q
B E K A G H O W I C F T E V X H A J L H S C T F L
F Y H C Z S P L J O M L Y R Z P M K J Y F G I M L
S C S B J L P D S H N P V J X G N Z E Q G W O W Y
R S J M B F E P G K S T R B Z S R B T R Z Y N M G
R L W K X H R H Q P F Z X H Z T P L Y M C L K G Q
```

BELLE	DOOM	IGNORANCE	NEPHEW	TIM
BLACK	EBENEZER	INVITATION	PAST	TOPPER
CAP	EVE	JACOB	PETER	TURKEY
CHAINS	FAN	JOE	PRESENT	UNDERTAKER
CHARWOMAN	FEZZIWIG	KNOCKER	RECLAMATION	WANT
CHRISTMAS	FRED	LAUNDRESS	SCRATCH	WAREHOUSE
CRATCHIT	GRAVE	LONDON	SCROOGE	WHITE
DICKENS	GREEN	MARLEY	SCUTTLE	
DILBER	HUMBUG	MARTHA	TAVERN	

A Christmas Carol Word Search 3 Answer Key

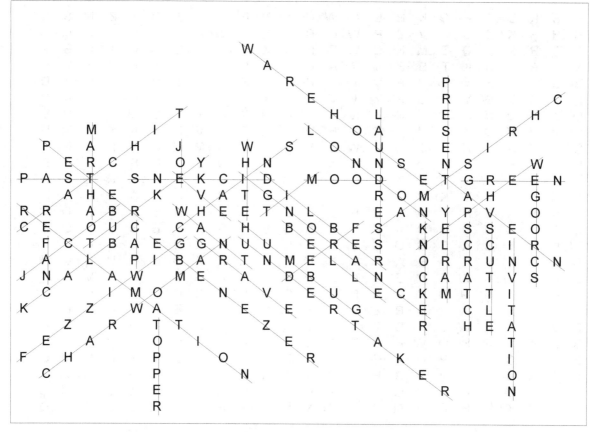

BELLE	DOOM	IGNORANCE	NEPHEW	TIM
BLACK	EBENEZER	INVITATION	PAST	TOPPER
CAP	EVE	JACOB	PETER	TURKEY
CHAINS	FAN	JOE	PRESENT	UNDERTAKER
CHARWOMAN	FEZZIWIG	KNOCKER	RECLAMATION	WANT
CHRISTMAS	FRED	LAUNDRESS	SCRATCH	WAREHOUSE
CRATCHIT	GRAVE	LONDON	SCROOGE	WHITE
DICKENS	GREEN	MARLEY	SCUTTLE	
DILBER	HUMBUG	MARTHA	TAVERN	

```
K N P Q K Q L G S B V R H C F Z M W D Y W N D W P
S K V N Y Q R C D T P R Q H Q S A C Y H M V Z S V
C R M D V M X Q Y Z T R T R D B R L I M B B R W Y
V S K L U N J B F T B H E I Q D L T H F F T M K B
V R T Q N E W D Q B S T C S F R E D B E L L E P J
V J Y C D P T C F L Q Q N T E P Y Y F Z J X E E J
R A D T E H W X W Q H I P M L N N X P M C Q B T C
J C N H R E Q R N U A R P A D Y T N B F A W E E C
D O O M T W T I M H T R E S D I L B E R P T N R Z
Y B E C A D A B C Z Z V C C C W D A Y P S O E E J
V P K N K D U N C D E R H S L R A F U A Z P Z L V
J B I G E G T F T R A X J W N A O R P N J P E T B
F A N G R E E N E T A V E R N B M O E L D E R T M
Z D V T N A M Q C Z U T N L S L L A G H O R H U M
G S I C Q P V H N Q Z R C Z C A Y R T E O N E C Q
T G T C B T B E A D M I K H L C S K F I S U D S F
R V A C K M V H R D A R W E I K B C M N O G S O S
C L T D N E F K O S R W T I Y T J K A F K N L E N
F M I N R V N Z N D T D X W G L W M B C Z V C H Z
L M O N V O Q S G K H D J H B R O Y S L L F W J X
K Y N D C N S C I N A S W C Y W R R J K T C M T
D Y H K D B W P C L M P D L R C V H C Z W Q G B S
C S E C P C D M G K P K R A R L N M F W F J D Q S
Q R W Y V L Q J H R B Q H M T T K T R F N S D M H
X G M F H M F F H G L C H V H W V C F D W X K H X
```

BELLE	DOOM	IGNORANCE	NEPHEW	TIM
BLACK	EBENEZER	INVITATION	PAST	TOPPER
CAP	EVE	JACOB	PETER	TURKEY
CHAINS	FAN	JOE	PRESENT	UNDERTAKER
CHARWOMAN	FEZZIWIG	KNOCKER	RECLAMATION	WANT
CHRISTMAS	FRED	LAUNDRESS	SCRATCH	WAREHOUSE
CRATCHIT	GRAVE	LONDON	SCROOGE	WHITE
DICKENS	GREEN	MARLEY	SCUTTLE	
DILBER	HUMBUG	MARTHA	TAVERN	

A Christmas Carol Word Search 4 Answer Key

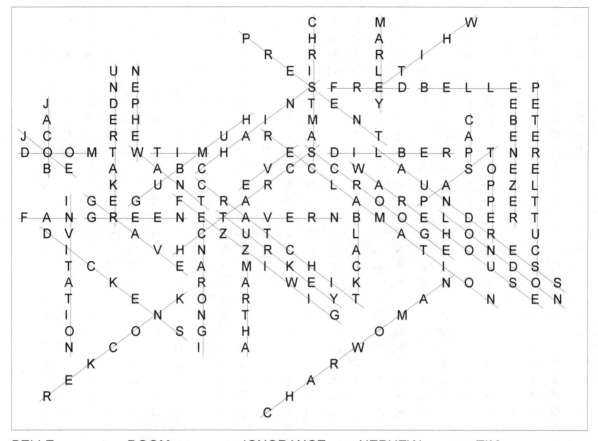

BELLE	DOOM	IGNORANCE	NEPHEW	TIM
BLACK	EBENEZER	INVITATION	PAST	TOPPER
CAP	EVE	JACOB	PETER	TURKEY
CHAINS	FAN	JOE	PRESENT	UNDERTAKER
CHARWOMAN	FEZZIWIG	KNOCKER	RECLAMATION	WANT
CHRISTMAS	FRED	LAUNDRESS	SCRATCH	WAREHOUSE
CRATCHIT	GRAVE	LONDON	SCROOGE	WHITE
DICKENS	GREEN	MARLEY	SCUTTLE	
DILBER	HUMBUG	MARTHA	TAVERN	

A Christmas Carol Crossword 1

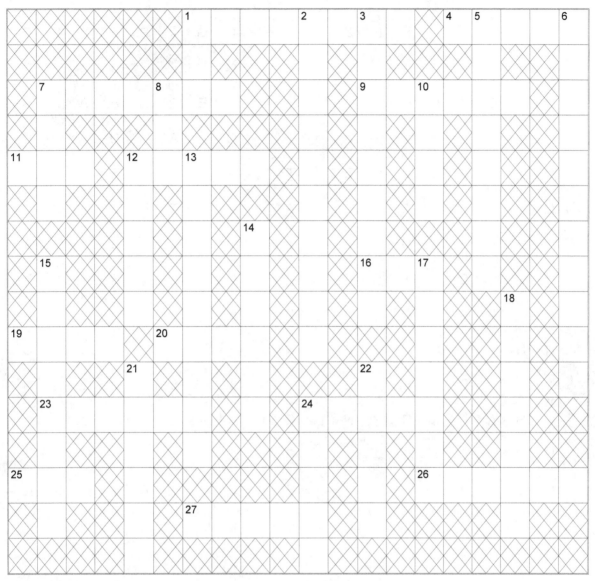

Across
1. Scrooge's former master
4. Cratchit's older son, looking for a job
7. Author
9. Invited Scrooge to Christmas dinner
11. Old man looking at Scrooge's things
12. Scrooge's former fiancee
16. Worn by first Spirit: extinguisher ___
19. The girl under the spirit's robe
20. Scrooge's nephew
23. Marley was wearing the ones he forged in life
24. Last spirit showed Scrooge his name on a ___ stone
25. Cratchit's lame youngest son: Tiny ___
26. Where Scrooge ate
27. Tunic color of the Spirit of Christmas Past

Down
1. Scrooge's sister
2. Good afternoon was Scrooge's reply to his nephew's ___
3. The boy under the spirit's robe

5. Scrooge's first name
6. What first spirit came for
7. Written on the boy's brow
8. When Marley appeared: Christmas ___
10. White hair; face without wrinkles
12. Garment color of Spirit of Christmas Yet To Come
13. Mrs. Dilber's job
14. Setting of novel
15. Scrooge's clerk Bob
17. Said Tiny Tim might die
18. It turned into Marley's face
21. Laundress who took Scrooge's things
22. Marley's first name
24. Robe color of Spirit of Christmas Present

A Christmas Carol Crossword 1 Answer Key

1	2	3	4	5	6	7	8	9	10	11	12	13	14	15	16	17	18	19
					1 F	E	Z	Z	2 I	W	3 I	G		4 P	5 E	T	E	6 R
					A				N		G				B			E
7 D	I	C	K	8 E	N	S			V		9 N	E	10 P	H	E	W		C
O				V					I		O		A		N			L
11 J	O	E	12 B	E	13 L	L	E		T		R		S		E			A
M			L		A				T		A		T		Z			M
			A		U		14 L		T		N				E			A
15 C			C		N		O		I		16 C	A	17 P		R			T
R			K		D		N		O		E		R		18 K			I
19 W	A	N	T	20 F	R	E	D		N				E		N			O
T			21 D		E		O		22 J				S		O			N
23 C	H	A	I	N	S		N				24 G	R	A	V	E			C
H			L		S						R		C		N			K
25 T	I	M	B		E		O						26 T	A	V	E	R	N
T			E		27 W	H	I	T	E		B					R		
			R								N							

Across
1. Scrooge's former master
4. Cratchit's older son, looking for a job
7. Author
9. Invited Scrooge to Christmas dinner
11. Old man looking at Scrooge's things
12. Scrooge's former fiancee
16. Worn by first Spirit: extinguisher ___
19. The girl under the spirit's robe
20. Scrooge's nephew
23. Marley was wearing the ones he forged in life
24. Last spirit showed Scrooge his name on a ___ stone
25. Cratchit's lame youngest son: Tiny ___
26. Where Scrooge ate
27. Tunic color of the Spirit of Christmas Past

Down
1. Scrooge's sister
2. Good afternoon was Scrooge's reply to his nephew's ___
3. The boy under the spirit's robe
5. Scrooge's first name
6. What first spirit came for
7. Written on the boy's brow
8. When Marley appeared: Christmas ___
10. White hair; face without wrinkles
12. Garment color of Spirit of Christmas Yet To Come
13. Mrs. Dilber's job
14. Setting of novel
15. Scrooge's clerk Bob
17. Said Tiny Tim might die
18. It turned into Marley's face
21. Laundress who took Scrooge's things
22. Marley's first name
24. Robe color of Spirit of Christmas Present

A Christmas Carol Crossword 2

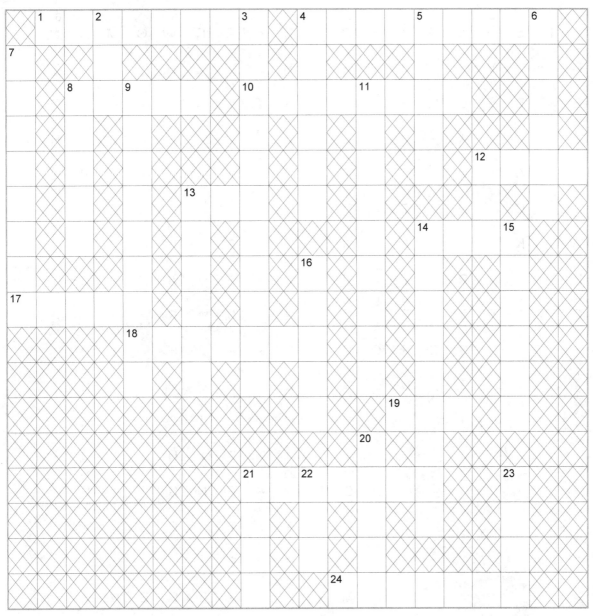

Across
1. Scrooge's first name
4. Took Scrooge's bed curtains
8. Scrooge's former fiancee
10. Scrooge's clerk Bob
12. Scrooge's nephew
13. Cratchit's lame youngest son: Tiny ___
14. The girl under the spirit's robe
17. Last spirit showed Scrooge his name on a ___ stone
18. Covetous old sinner
19. Old man looking at Scrooge's things
21. Author
24. Said Tiny Tim might die

Down
2. When Marley appeared: Christmas ___
3. What first spirit came for

4. Marley was wearing the ones he forged in life
5. Tunic color of the Spirit of Christmas Past
6. Invited Scrooge to Christmas dinner
7. Scrooge's former master
8. Garment color of Spirit of Christmas Yet To Come
9. Mrs. Dilber's job
11. Scrooge did not miss it
12. Scrooge's sister
13. Where Scrooge ate
14. Scrooge's place of business
15. Pretended to be blind during the game
16. Robe color of Spirit of Christmas Present
20. Cratchit's older son, looking for a job
21. Written on the boy's brow
22. Worn by first Spirit: extinguisher ___
23. White hair; face without wrinkles

A Christmas Carol Crossword 2 Answer Key

1	2	3	4	5	6	7	8	9	10	11	12	13	14	15	16	17	18	19	20
	(1)E	B	(2)E	N	E	Z	E	(3)R		(4)C	H	A	R	(5)W	O	M	A	(6)N	
	(7)F		V					E		H				H				E	
	E	(8)B	E	(9)L	L	E		(10)C	R	A	T	(11)C	H	I	T			P	
	Z	L		A				L		I		H		T				H	
	Z	A		U				A		N		R		E		(12)F	R	E	D
	I			N		(13)T	I	M		S		I				A		W	
	W	K		D		A		A				S		(14)W	A	N	(15)T		
	I			R		V		T		(16)G		T		A			O		
	(17)G	R	A	V	E	E		I		R		M		R			P		
				(18)S	C	R	O	O	G	E		A		E			P		
				S		N		N		E		S		H			E		
										N			(19)J	O	E		R		
												(20)P		U					
								(21)D	I	(22)C	K	E	N	S				(23)P	
								O		A		T		E				A	
								O		P		E		S				S	
								M			(24)P	R	E	S	E	N	T	T	

Across
1. Scrooge's first name
4. Took Scrooge's bed curtains
8. Scrooge's former fiancee
10. Scrooge's clerk Bob
12. Scrooge's nephew
13. Cratchit's lame youngest son: Tiny ___
14. The girl under the spirit's robe
17. Last spirit showed Scrooge his name on a ___ stone
18. Covetous old sinner
19. Old man looking at Scrooge's things
21. Author
24. Said Tiny Tim might die

Down
2. When Marley appeared: Christmas ___
3. What first spirit came for
4. Marley was wearing the ones he forged in life
5. Tunic color of the Spirit of Christmas Past
6. Invited Scrooge to Christmas dinner
7. Scrooge's former master
8. Garment color of Spirit of Christmas Yet To Come
9. Mrs. Dilber's job
11. Scrooge did not miss it
12. Scrooge's sister
13. Where Scrooge ate
14. Scrooge's place of business
15. Pretended to be blind during the game
16. Robe color of Spirit of Christmas Present
20. Cratchit's older son, looking for a job
21. Written on the boy's brow
22. Worn by first Spirit: extinguisher ___
23. White hair; face without wrinkles

A Christmas Carol Crossword 3

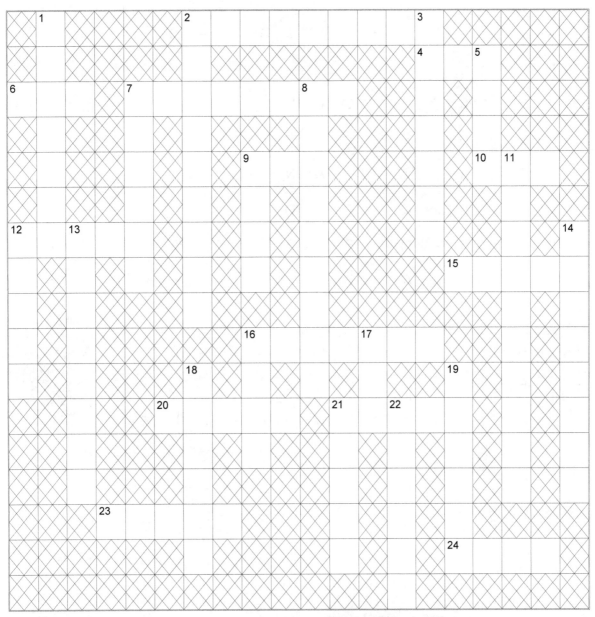

Across

2. Scrooge did not miss it
4. Worn by first Spirit: extinguisher ___
6. Old man looking at Scrooge's things
7. Scrooge's clerk Bob
9. Scrooge's sister
10. Cratchit's lame youngest son: Tiny ___
12. Robe color of Spirit of Christmas Present
15. Tunic color of the Spirit of Christmas Past
16. Author
20. Marley's first name
21. Scrooge's former fiancee
23. Cratchit's older son, looking for a job
24. The girl under the spirit's robe

Down

1. It turned into Marley's face

2. Took Scrooge's bed curtains
3. Scrooge told Bob to buy a new coal ___
5. White hair; face without wrinkles
7. Marley was wearing the ones he forged in life
8. The boy under the spirit's robe
9. Scrooge's nephew
11. Good afternoon was Scrooge's reply to his nephew's ___
12. Last spirit showed Scrooge his name on a ___ stone
13. Scrooge's first name
14. Scrooge's former master
16. Written on the boy's brow
17. When Marley appeared: Christmas ___
18. Dead partner
19. Invited Scrooge to Christmas dinner
21. Garment color of Spirit of Christmas Yet To Come
22. Setting of novel

A Christmas Carol Crossword 3 Answer Key

Completed grid (filled-in answers, by clue number):

Across: 2 CHRISTMAS · 4 CAP · 6 JOE · 7 CRATCHIT · 9 FAN · 10 TIM · 12 GREEN · 15 WHITE · 16 DICKENS · 20 JACOB · 21 BELLE · 23 PETER · 24 WANT

Down: 1 KNOCKER · 2 CHARWOMAN · 3 SCUTTLE · 5 PAST · 7 CHAINS · 8 IGNORANCE · 9 FRED · 11 INVITATION · 12 GRAVE · 13 EBENEZER · 14 FEZZIWIG · 16 DOOM · 17 EVE · 18 MARLEY · 19 NEPHEW · 21 BLACK · 22 LONDON

Across

2. Scrooge did not miss it
4. Worn by first Spirit: extinguisher ___
6. Old man looking at Scrooge's things
7. Scrooge's clerk Bob
9. Scrooge's sister
10. Cratchit's lame youngest son: Tiny ___
12. Robe color of Spirit of Christmas Present
15. Tunic color of the Spirit of Christmas Past
16. Author
20. Marley's first name
21. Scrooge's former fiancee
23. Cratchit's older son, looking for a job
24. The girl under the spirit's robe

Down

1. It turned into Marley's face
2. Took Scrooge's bed curtains
3. Scrooge told Bob to buy a new coal ___
5. White hair; face without wrinkles
7. Marley was wearing the ones he forged in life
8. The boy under the spirit's robe
9. Scrooge's nephew
11. Good afternoon was Scrooge's reply to his nephew's ___
12. Last spirit showed Scrooge his name on a ___ stone
13. Scrooge's first name
14. Scrooge's former master
16. Written on the boy's brow
17. When Marley appeared: Christmas ___
18. Dead partner
19. Invited Scrooge to Christmas dinner
21. Garment color of Spirit of Christmas Yet To Come
22. Setting of novel

A Christmas Carol Crossword 4

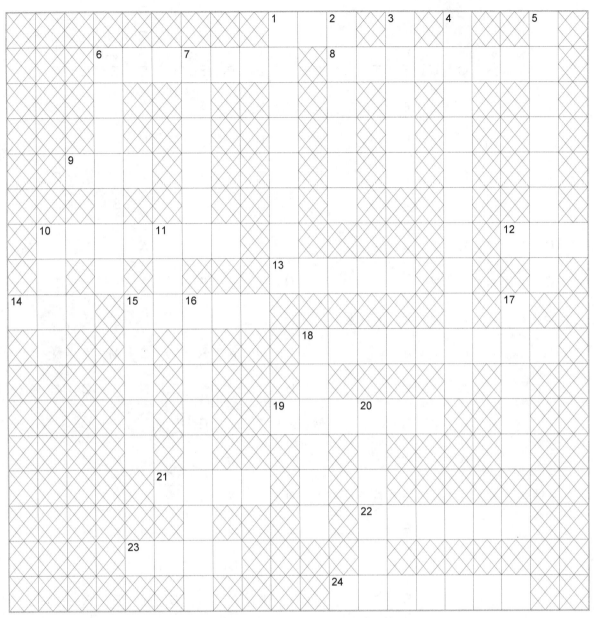

Across
1. Scrooge's sister
6. Scrooge told Bob to buy a new coal ___
8. Scrooge's first name
9. Worn by first Spirit: extinguisher ___
10. Author
12. Cratchit's lame youngest son: Tiny ___
13. Last spirit showed Scrooge his name on a ___ stone
14. Old man looking at Scrooge's things
15. Scrooge's former fiancee
18. Took Scrooge's bed curtains
19. Dead partner
21. Scrooge's nephew
22. Laundress who took Scrooge's things
23. White hair; face without wrinkles
24. It turned into Marley's face

Down
1. Scrooge's former master
2. Invited Scrooge to Christmas dinner
3. Cratchit's older son, looking for a job
4. What first spirit came for
5. Scrooge's clerk Bob
6. Nickname for the dead businessman: Old ___
7. Where Scrooge ate
10. Written on the boy's brow
11. When Marley appeared: Christmas ___
15. Garment color of Spirit of Christmas Yet To Come
16. Mrs. Dilber's job
17. Marley's first name
18. Marley was wearing the ones he forged in life
20. Setting of novel

A Christmas Carol Crossword 4 Answer Key

				1 F	A	N	2 N		3 P		4 R			5 C
	6 S	C	U	7 T	T	L	E		8 E	B	E	N	E	Z	E	R
		C		A			Z		P		T		C		A
		R		V			Z		H		E		L		T
	9 C	A	P	E			I		E		R		A		C
		T		R			W		W				M		H
10 D	I	C	K	11 E	N	S		I					12 T	I	M
	O		H		V			13 G	R	A	V	E		A		T
14 J	O	E		15 B	E	16 L	L	E						17 J
	M			L		A		18 C	H	A	R	W	O	M	A	N
				A		U		H				N		C
				C		N		19 M	A	20 R	L	E	Y		O
				K		D		I		O				B
			21 F	R	E	D		N		N			
				E				S		22 D	I	L	B	E	R
		23 P	A	S	T				O
			S				24 K	N	O	C	K	E	R

Across
1. Scrooge's sister
6. Scrooge told Bob to buy a new coal ___
8. Scrooge's first name
9. Worn by first Spirit: extinguisher ___
10. Author
12. Cratchit's lame youngest son: Tiny ___
13. Last spirit showed Scrooge his name on a ___ stone
14. Old man looking at Scrooge's things
15. Scrooge's former fiancee
18. Took Scrooge's bed curtains
19. Dead partner
21. Scrooge's nephew
22. Laundress who took Scrooge's things
23. White hair; face without wrinkles
24. It turned into Marley's face

Down
1. Scrooge's former master
2. Invited Scrooge to Christmas dinner
3. Cratchit's older son, looking for a job
4. What first spirit came for
5. Scrooge's clerk Bob
6. Nickname for the dead businessman: Old ___
7. Where Scrooge ate
10. Written on the boy's brow
11. When Marley appeared: Christmas ___
15. Garment color of Spirit of Christmas Yet To Come
16. Mrs. Dilber's job
17. Marley's first name
18. Marley was wearing the ones he forged in life
20. Setting of novel

CHRISTMAS CAROL UNIT

DOOM	HUMBUG	UNDERTAKER	SCROOGE	MARLEY
PRESENT	CAP	DILBER	CRATCHIT	CHAINS
WHITE	NEPHEW	FREE SPACE	TURKEY	CHRISTMAS
GREEN	GRAVE	SCRATCH	BLACK	TIM
MARTHA	EBENEZER	PETER	WANT	KNOCKER

CHRISTMAS CAROL UNIT

FAN	DICKENS	JACOB	TOPPER	INVITATION
JOE	LONDON	RECLAMATION	LAUNDRESS	CHARWOMAN
TAVERN	SCUTTLE	FREE SPACE	IGNORANCE	FEZZIWIG
BELLE	WAREHOUSE	FRED	KNOCKER	WANT
PETER	EBENEZER	MARTHA	TIM	BLACK

CHRISTMAS CAROL UNIT

EVE	TURKEY	WAREHOUSE	TAVERN	UNDERTAKER
INVITATION	SCROOGE	KNOCKER	PETER	JOE
BELLE	FRED	FREE SPACE	CRATCHIT	FAN
CHRISTMAS	JACOB	TIM	PAST	TOPPER
BLACK	DILBER	WHITE	HUMBUG	DICKENS

CHRISTMAS CAROL UNIT

MARTHA	FEZZIWIG	MARLEY	GREEN	SCUTTLE
RECLAMATION	LONDON	EBENEZER	IGNORANCE	CHAINS
CHARWOMAN	SCRATCH	FREE SPACE	WANT	NEPHEW
CAP	DOOM	LAUNDRESS	DICKENS	HUMBUG
WHITE	DILBER	BLACK	TOPPER	PAST

CHRISTMAS CAROL UNIT

WHITE	KNOCKER	DICKENS	JACOB	GRAVE
NEPHEW	PAST	RECLAMATION	TIM	FAN
EBENEZER	DILBER	FREE SPACE	BELLE	TAVERN
CHRISTMAS	SCUTTLE	TURKEY	MARLEY	MARTHA
HUMBUG	WANT	FEZZIWIG	DOOM	CHARWOMAN

CHRISTMAS CAROL UNIT

EVE	CAP	GREEN	TOPPER	SCROOGE
SCRATCH	LAUNDRESS	WAREHOUSE	PETER	INVITATION
FRED	BLACK	FREE SPACE	CHAINS	CRATCHIT
IGNORANCE	JOE	UNDERTAKER	CHARWOMAN	DOOM
FEZZIWIG	WANT	HUMBUG	MARTHA	MARLEY

CHRISTMAS CAROL UNIT

TOPPER	MARTHA	SCUTTLE	WHITE	NEPHEW
TIM	LONDON	CHRISTMAS	INVITATION	FAN
FEZZIWIG	CHAINS	FREE SPACE	CRATCHIT	GREEN
SCRATCH	PAST	RECLAMATION	CHARWOMAN	MARLEY
PETER	WAREHOUSE	EBENEZER	DOOM	EVE

CHRISTMAS CAROL UNIT

TAVERN	PRESENT	WANT	LAUNDRESS	FRED
IGNORANCE	KNOCKER	SCROOGE	DILBER	DICKENS
TURKEY	HUMBUG	FREE SPACE	JOE	GRAVE
BELLE	JACOB	BLACK	EVE	DOOM
EBENEZER	WAREHOUSE	PETER	MARLEY	CHARWOMAN

CHRISTMAS CAROL UNIT

FAN	CHAINS	BELLE	BLACK	FRED
PETER	IGNORANCE	LAUNDRESS	GREEN	DOOM
TURKEY	DICKENS	FREE SPACE	HUMBUG	EBENEZER
JOE	TOPPER	FEZZIWIG	PRESENT	MARLEY
WHITE	CAP	EVE	KNOCKER	MARTHA

CHRISTMAS CAROL UNIT

SCUTTLE	INVITATION	CHARWOMAN	LONDON	UNDERTAKER
TIM	JACOB	RECLAMATION	SCROOGE	WAREHOUSE
DILBER	WANT	FREE SPACE	NEPHEW	TAVERN
CRATCHIT	PAST	SCRATCH	MARTHA	KNOCKER
EVE	CAP	WHITE	MARLEY	PRESENT

CHRISTMAS CAROL UNIT

PRESENT	TURKEY	TOPPER	MARLEY	EVE
HUMBUG	PETER	LONDON	BLACK	UNDERTAKER
DILBER	CRATCHIT	FREE SPACE	FRED	KNOCKER
FAN	NEPHEW	JOE	CAP	GREEN
CHAINS	TAVERN	TIM	WHITE	WAREHOUSE

CHRISTMAS CAROL UNIT

JACOB	CHRISTMAS	IGNORANCE	SCROOGE	MARTHA
INVITATION	RECLAMATION	DICKENS	GRAVE	DOOM
SCRATCH	PAST	FREE SPACE	FEZZIWIG	LAUNDRESS
WANT	EBENEZER	SCUTTLE	WAREHOUSE	WHITE
TIM	TAVERN	CHAINS	GREEN	CAP

CHRISTMAS CAROL UNIT

DOOM	BELLE	RECLAMATION	TAVERN	CHRISTMAS
IGNORANCE	BLACK	CAP	CRATCHIT	DILBER
LONDON	PETER	FREE SPACE	WAREHOUSE	TIM
FAN	LAUNDRESS	INVITATION	TURKEY	HUMBUG
EVE	TOPPER	WANT	DICKENS	NEPHEW

CHRISTMAS CAROL UNIT

SCUTTLE	UNDERTAKER	GREEN	EBENEZER	PRESENT
JACOB	PAST	SCRATCH	MARLEY	WHITE
FRED	CHAINS	FREE SPACE	GRAVE	FEZZIWIG
MARTHA	KNOCKER	SCROOGE	NEPHEW	DICKENS
WANT	TOPPER	EVE	HUMBUG	TURKEY

51

CHRISTMAS CAROL UNIT

FRED	WAREHOUSE	PAST	KNOCKER	DILBER
CHAINS	JACOB	FEZZIWIG	WHITE	CRATCHIT
IGNORANCE	WANT	FREE SPACE	PRESENT	TOPPER
SCRATCH	EVE	BLACK	PETER	BELLE
TIM	CAP	MARLEY	CHARWOMAN	TURKEY

CHRISTMAS CAROL UNIT

INVITATION	TAVERN	NEPHEW	UNDERTAKER	DICKENS
EBENEZER	SCROOGE	LAUNDRESS	FAN	MARTHA
SCUTTLE	DOOM	FREE SPACE	CHRISTMAS	JOE
HUMBUG	GRAVE	RECLAMATION	TURKEY	CHARWOMAN
MARLEY	CAP	TIM	BELLE	PETER

CHRISTMAS CAROL UNIT

DILBER	JACOB	TAVERN	FAN	WANT
NEPHEW	CRATCHIT	WAREHOUSE	HUMBUG	MARLEY
PRESENT	MARTHA	FREE SPACE	DICKENS	RECLAMATION
CAP	SCUTTLE	FEZZIWIG	LAUNDRESS	FRED
BELLE	WHITE	EBENEZER	CHARWOMAN	SCRATCH

CHRISTMAS CAROL UNIT

CHRISTMAS	KNOCKER	SCROOGE	EVE	PAST
LONDON	JOE	GREEN	BLACK	INVITATION
CHAINS	TOPPER	FREE SPACE	DOOM	IGNORANCE
TIM	UNDERTAKER	TURKEY	SCRATCH	CHARWOMAN
EBENEZER	WHITE	BELLE	FRED	LAUNDRESS

CHRISTMAS CAROL UNIT

HUMBUG	JOE	KNOCKER	SCRATCH	IGNORANCE
EVE	SCUTTLE	PAST	RECLAMATION	UNDERTAKER
GRAVE	NEPHEW	FREE SPACE	TOPPER	WANT
LONDON	TIM	PETER	TURKEY	WAREHOUSE
CRATCHIT	DICKENS	DOOM	DILBER	GREEN

CHRISTMAS CAROL UNIT

LAUNDRESS	MARLEY	BLACK	CAP	BELLE
EBENEZER	CHAINS	CHRISTMAS	INVITATION	FRED
MARTHA	JACOB	FREE SPACE	FAN	TAVERN
FEZZIWIG	SCROOGE	WHITE	GREEN	DILBER
DOOM	DICKENS	CRATCHIT	WAREHOUSE	TURKEY

CHRISTMAS CAROL UNIT

FRED	SCRATCH	DILBER	SCUTTLE	IGNORANCE
CHAINS	CHARWOMAN	UNDERTAKER	EBENEZER	BELLE
FAN	CHRISTMAS	FREE SPACE	HUMBUG	WAREHOUSE
DICKENS	SCROOGE	FEZZIWIG	WHITE	WANT
TAVERN	BLACK	RECLAMATION	MARTHA	INVITATION

CHRISTMAS CAROL UNIT

NEPHEW	TOPPER	LAUNDRESS	CRATCHIT	JACOB
TIM	PRESENT	CAP	LONDON	TURKEY
EVE	PAST	FREE SPACE	JOE	DOOM
KNOCKER	MARLEY	PETER	INVITATION	MARTHA
RECLAMATION	BLACK	TAVERN	WANT	WHITE

CHRISTMAS CAROL UNIT

JACOB	WHITE	MARTHA	BLACK	FRED
TURKEY	WANT	BELLE	LAUNDRESS	TAVERN
LONDON	CHAINS	FREE SPACE	KNOCKER	GRAVE
UNDERTAKER	MARLEY	TOPPER	INVITATION	IGNORANCE
WAREHOUSE	CRATCHIT	CHRISTMAS	FEZZIWIG	FAN

CHRISTMAS CAROL UNIT

SCUTTLE	SCROOGE	DICKENS	TIM	JOE
PAST	EVE	CHARWOMAN	SCRATCH	DILBER
EBENEZER	PETER	FREE SPACE	NEPHEW	CAP
DOOM	PRESENT	HUMBUG	FAN	FEZZIWIG
CHRISTMAS	CRATCHIT	WAREHOUSE	IGNORANCE	INVITATION

CHRISTMAS CAROL UNIT

BELLE	MARLEY	RECLAMATION	CAP	WHITE
CHAINS	KNOCKER	EBENEZER	MARTHA	WAREHOUSE
INVITATION	CHARWOMAN	FREE SPACE	PAST	DILBER
SCUTTLE	NEPHEW	TOPPER	GREEN	TAVERN
JACOB	LONDON	JOE	BLACK	GRAVE

CHRISTMAS CAROL UNIT

PETER	FAN	HUMBUG	EVE	UNDERTAKER
SCRATCH	TURKEY	WANT	SCROOGE	FEZZIWIG
CHRISTMAS	DICKENS	FREE SPACE	FRED	PRESENT
DOOM	CRATCHIT	TIM	GRAVE	BLACK
JOE	LONDON	JACOB	TAVERN	GREEN

CHRISTMAS CAROL UNIT

CHARWOMAN	LONDON	LAUNDRESS	TIM	PETER
CAP	TURKEY	CHRISTMAS	TAVERN	GRAVE
UNDERTAKER	BELLE	FREE SPACE	CRATCHIT	JACOB
DILBER	FEZZIWIG	INVITATION	SCUTTLE	PRESENT
BLACK	NEPHEW	TOPPER	CHAINS	WANT

CHRISTMAS CAROL UNIT

FAN	GREEN	FRED	JOE	DOOM
SCRATCH	RECLAMATION	WHITE	EBENEZER	PAST
KNOCKER	DICKENS	FREE SPACE	MARLEY	EVE
WAREHOUSE	SCROOGE	IGNORANCE	WANT	CHAINS
TOPPER	NEPHEW	BLACK	PRESENT	SCUTTLE

CHRISTMAS CAROL UNIT

EBENEZER	DILBER	WANT	JOE	SCROOGE
HUMBUG	TAVERN	CHAINS	WHITE	MARLEY
BELLE	LONDON	FREE SPACE	CHARWOMAN	TOPPER
KNOCKER	SCRATCH	FAN	IGNORANCE	DICKENS
CHRISTMAS	JACOB	SCUTTLE	CRATCHIT	PETER

CHRISTMAS CAROL UNIT

EVE	TURKEY	PRESENT	BLACK	FEZZIWIG
GRAVE	FRED	TIM	DOOM	WAREHOUSE
NEPHEW	GREEN	FREE SPACE	LAUNDRESS	MARTHA
RECLAMATION	CAP	INVITATION	PETER	CRATCHIT
SCUTTLE	JACOB	CHRISTMAS	DICKENS	IGNORANCE

59

CHRISTMAS CAROL UNIT

GRAVE	TAVERN	DILBER	LAUNDRESS	KNOCKER
DICKENS	WHITE	TURKEY	CHRISTMAS	TIM
CHAINS	MARLEY	FREE SPACE	NEPHEW	PAST
TOPPER	UNDERTAKER	RECLAMATION	BELLE	SCUTTLE
WAREHOUSE	FEZZIWIG	CRATCHIT	IGNORANCE	HUMBUG

CHRISTMAS CAROL UNIT

BLACK	CHARWOMAN	MARTHA	INVITATION	PETER
EBENEZER	JACOB	PRESENT	EVE	WANT
CAP	GREEN	FREE SPACE	FRED	DOOM
SCRATCH	FAN	SCROOGE	HUMBUG	IGNORANCE
CRATCHIT	FEZZIWIG	WAREHOUSE	SCUTTLE	BELLE

Christmas Carol Vocabulary Word List

No.	Word	Clue/Definition
1.	ABSTINENCE	Avoidance
2.	ADVERSARY	Opponent; enemy
3.	AGITATED	Stirred up; disturbed
4.	ALTERATION	Change
5.	BENEVOLENCE	Generosity; kindness
6.	BLITHE	Joyous; happy
7.	CAPACIOUS	Spacious; large
8.	CONDESCENSION	Being courteous with a superior air
9.	CONSOLATION	Comfort; compassion
10.	CORDIALLY	Graciously; in a friendly way
11.	COVETOUS	Desirous of what someone else has
12.	DESTITUTE	Poor; penniless
13.	DETESTATION	Intense dislike
14.	DISDAINING	Treating with scorn or contempt
15.	DISPELLED	Scattered; caused to vanish
16.	ENCOMPASS	Surround
17.	ESSENCE	Spirit
18.	EXECRABLE	Very bad; offensive
19.	EXTRAVAGANCE	Extremely abundant; excessive
20.	FACETIOUS	Humorous; merry
21.	FEIGN	Pretend
22.	FETTERED	Shackled; chained
23.	ILLUSTRIOUS	Glorious; brilliant
24.	INEXORABLE	Relentless; unyielding
25.	INFAMOUS	Well-known for bad reasons
26.	INTERCEDES	Pleads on another's behalf
27.	KINDRED	Related; belonging to the same family
28.	LATENT	Dormant; hidden
29.	LIVID	Angry; furious
30.	LOITER	Hang around; linger
31.	MELANCHOLY	Sadness; depression; gloom
32.	MOROSE	Ill-humored; sullen
33.	OBSCURE	Dark; vague; unclear
34.	ODIOUS	Hateful
35.	OFFICIOUS	Meddlesome; self-important
36.	OMINOUS	Threatening
37.	PEDESTRIAN	Going on foot; walking
38.	PORTLY	Stout; fat
39.	PRECEPTS	Practical rules guiding conduct
40.	PRODIGIOUSLY	Enormously; hugely
41.	RECOMPENSED	Repaid
42.	RECUMBENT	Reclining; lying down
43.	RELENTS	Softens in attitude or temper
44.	REMONSTRATED	Protested
45.	RESOLUTE	Determined
46.	SORDID	Filthy; vile
47.	SUPPLICATION	Asking for humbly or earnestly
48.	SUSCEPTIBLE	Impressionable; easily influenced
49.	UBIQUITOUS	Being everywhere
50.	UNANIMITY	Complete agreement

_____ 1. Glorious; brilliant

_____ 2. Impressionable; easily influenced

_____ 3. Protested

_____ 4. Enormously; hugely

_____ 5. Going on foot; walking

_____ 6. Stout; fat

_____ 7. Softens in attitude or temper

_____ 8. Relentless; unyielding

_____ 9. Extremely abundant; excessive

_____ 10. Pleads on another's behalf

_____ 11. Opponent; enemy

_____ 12. Dark; vague; unclear

_____ 13. Generosity; kindness

_____ 14. Reclining; lying down

_____ 15. Sadness; depression; gloom

_____ 16. Related; belonging to the same family

_____ 17. Determined

_____ 18. Being everywhere

_____ 19. Being courteous with a superior air

_____ 20. Hang around; linger

ILLUSTRIOUS	1. Glorious; brilliant
SUSCEPTIBLE	2. Impressionable; easily influenced
REMONSTRATED	3. Protested
PRODIGIOUSLY	4. Enormously; hugely
PEDESTRIAN	5. Going on foot; walking
PORTLY	6. Stout; fat
RELENTS	7. Softens in attitude or temper
INEXORABLE	8. Relentless; unyielding
EXTRAVAGANCE	9. Extremely abundant; excessive
INTERCEDES	10. Pleads on another's behalf
ADVERSARY	11. Opponent; enemy
OBSCURE	12. Dark; vague; unclear
BENEVOLENCE	13. Generosity; kindness
RECUMBENT	14. Reclining; lying down
MELANCHOLY	15. Sadness; depression; gloom
KINDRED	16. Related; belonging to the same family
RESOLUTE	17. Determined
UBIQUITOUS	18. Being everywhere
CONDESCENSION	19. Being courteous with a superior air
LOITER	20. Hang around; linger

A Christmas Carol Vocabulary Fill In The Blank 2

_____ 1. Extremely abundant; excessive

_____ 2. Desirous of what someone else has

_____ 3. Pretend

_____ 4. Related; belonging to the same family

_____ 5. Avoidance

_____ 6. Ill-humored; sullen

_____ 7. Stout; fat

_____ 8. Joyous; happy

_____ 9. Spirit

_____ 10. Change

_____ 11. Scattered; caused to vanish

_____ 12. Meddlesome; self-important

_____ 13. Dark; vague; unclear

_____ 14. Relentless; unyielding

_____ 15. Intense dislike

_____ 16. Being everywhere

_____ 17. Glorious; brilliant

_____ 18. Angry; furious

_____ 19. Generosity; kindness

_____ 20. Impressionable; easily influenced

EXTRAVAGANCE	1. Extremely abundant; excessive
COVETOUS	2. Desirous of what someone else has
FEIGN	3. Pretend
KINDRED	4. Related; belonging to the same family
ABSTINENCE	5. Avoidance
MOROSE	6. Ill-humored; sullen
PORTLY	7. Stout; fat
BLITHE	8. Joyous; happy
ESSENCE	9. Spirit
ALTERATION	10. Change
DISPELLED	11. Scattered; caused to vanish
OFFICIOUS	12. Meddlesome; self-important
OBSCURE	13. Dark; vague; unclear
INEXORABLE	14. Relentless; unyielding
DETESTATION	15. Intense dislike
UBIQUITOUS	16. Being everywhere
ILLUSTRIOUS	17. Glorious; brilliant
LIVID	18. Angry; furious
BENEVOLENCE	19. Generosity; kindness
SUSCEPTIBLE	20. Impressionable; easily influenced

_____	1. Reclining; lying down
_____	2. Complete agreement
_____	3. Asking for humbly or earnestly
_____	4. Avoidance
_____	5. Pretend
_____	6. Spacious; large
_____	7. Humorous; merry
_____	8. Practical rules guiding conduct
_____	9. Desirous of what someone else has
_____	10. Surround
_____	11. Poor; penniless
_____	12. Opponent; enemy
_____	13. Hateful
_____	14. Graciously; in a friendly way
_____	15. Change
_____	16. Hang around; linger
_____	17. Very bad; offensive
_____	18. Going on foot; walking
_____	19. Related; belonging to the same family
_____	20. Being courteous with a superior air

RECUMBENT	1. Reclining; lying down
UNANIMITY	2. Complete agreement
SUPPLICATION	3. Asking for humbly or earnestly
ABSTINENCE	4. Avoidance
FEIGN	5. Pretend
CAPACIOUS	6. Spacious; large
FACETIOUS	7. Humorous; merry
PRECEPTS	8. Practical rules guiding conduct
COVETOUS	9. Desirous of what someone else has
ENCOMPASS	10. Surround
DESTITUTE	11. Poor; penniless
ADVERSARY	12. Opponent; enemy
ODIOUS	13. Hateful
CORDIALLY	14. Graciously; in a friendly way
ALTERATION	15. Change
LOITER	16. Hang around; linger
EXECRABLE	17. Very bad; offensive
PEDESTRIAN	18. Going on foot; walking
KINDRED	19. Related; belonging to the same family
CONDESCENSION	20. Being courteous with a superior air

A Christmas Carol Vocabulary Fill In The Blank 4

_____ 1. Change

_____ 2. Reclining; lying down

_____ 3. Enormously; hugely

_____ 4. Joyous; happy

_____ 5. Spacious; large

_____ 6. Pretend

_____ 7. Related; belonging to the same family

_____ 8. Threatening

_____ 9. Intense dislike

_____ 10. Relentless; unyielding

_____ 11. Ill-humored; sullen

_____ 12. Opponent; enemy

_____ 13. Angry; furious

_____ 14. Going on foot; walking

_____ 15. Graciously; in a friendly way

_____ 16. Sadness; depression; gloom

_____ 17. Shackled; chained

_____ 18. Meddlesome; self-important

_____ 19. Surround

_____ 20. Generosity; kindness

ALTERATION	1. Change
RECUMBENT	2. Reclining; lying down
PRODIGIOUSLY	3. Enormously; hugely
BLITHE	4. Joyous; happy
CAPACIOUS	5. Spacious; large
FEIGN	6. Pretend
KINDRED	7. Related; belonging to the same family
OMINOUS	8. Threatening
DETESTATION	9. Intense dislike
INEXORABLE	10. Relentless; unyielding
MOROSE	11. Ill-humored; sullen
ADVERSARY	12. Opponent; enemy
LIVID	13. Angry; furious
PEDESTRIAN	14. Going on foot; walking
CORDIALLY	15. Graciously; in a friendly way
MELANCHOLY	16. Sadness; depression; gloom
FETTERED	17. Shackled; chained
OFFICIOUS	18. Meddlesome; self-important
ENCOMPASS	19. Surround
BENEVOLENCE	20. Generosity; kindness

A Christmas Carol Vocabulary Matching 1

___ 1. PORTLY	A. Protested
___ 2. MOROSE	B. Ill-humored; sullen
___ 3. RECUMBENT	C. Repaid
___ 4. ILLUSTRIOUS	D. Filthy; vile
___ 5. INFAMOUS	E. Glorious; brilliant
___ 6. BENEVOLENCE	F. Determined
___ 7. FEIGN	G. Complete agreement
___ 8. PEDESTRIAN	H. Scattered; caused to vanish
___ 9. DESTITUTE	I. Pretend
___10. COVETOUS	J. Desirous of what someone else has
___11. EXTRAVAGANCE	K. Spacious; large
___12. FACETIOUS	L. Generosity; kindness
___13. ALTERATION	M. Well-known for bad reasons
___14. KINDRED	N. Pleads on another's behalf
___15. UNANIMITY	O. Extremely abundant; excessive
___16. OFFICIOUS	P. Opponent; enemy
___17. RESOLUTE	Q. Meddlesome; self-important
___18. CAPACIOUS	R. Hang around; linger
___19. LOITER	S. Going on foot; walking
___20. SORDID	T. Reclining; lying down
___21. INTERCEDES	U. Related; belonging to the same family
___22. RECOMPENSED	V. Change
___23. REMONSTRATED	W. Poor; penniless
___24. DISPELLED	X. Humorous; merry
___25. ADVERSARY	Y. Stout; fat

A Christmas Carol Vocabulary Matching 1 Answer Key

Y - 1. PORTLY
B - 2. MOROSE
T - 3. RECUMBENT
E - 4. ILLUSTRIOUS
M - 5. INFAMOUS
L - 6. BENEVOLENCE
I - 7. FEIGN
S - 8. PEDESTRIAN
W - 9. DESTITUTE
J - 10. COVETOUS
O -11. EXTRAVAGANCE
X -12. FACETIOUS
V -13. ALTERATION
U -14. KINDRED
G -15. UNANIMITY
Q -16. OFFICIOUS
F -17. RESOLUTE
K -18. CAPACIOUS
R -19. LOITER
D -20. SORDID
N -21. INTERCEDES
C -22. RECOMPENSED
A -23. REMONSTRATED
H -24. DISPELLED
P -25. ADVERSARY

A. Protested
B. Ill-humored; sullen
C. Repaid
D. Filthy; vile
E. Glorious; brilliant
F. Determined
G. Complete agreement
H. Scattered; caused to vanish
I. Pretend
J. Desirous of what someone else has
K. Spacious; large
L. Generosity; kindness
M. Well-known for bad reasons
N. Pleads on another's behalf
O. Extremely abundant; excessive
P. Opponent; enemy
Q. Meddlesome; self-important
R. Hang around; linger
S. Going on foot; walking
T. Reclining; lying down
U. Related; belonging to the same family
V. Change
W. Poor; penniless
X. Humorous; merry
Y. Stout; fat

A Christmas Carol Vocabulary Matching 2

___ 1. CONSOLATION	A. Determined
___ 2. ENCOMPASS	B. Treating with scorn or contempt
___ 3. INTERCEDES	C. Reclining; lying down
___ 4. DISDAINING	D. Sadness; depression; gloom
___ 5. OFFICIOUS	E. Generosity; kindness
___ 6. UNANIMITY	F. Meddlesome; self-important
___ 7. CONDESCENSION	G. Stout; fat
___ 8. LIVID	H. Angry; furious
___ 9. PEDESTRIAN	I. Surround
___10. BENEVOLENCE	J. Well-known for bad reasons
___11. INFAMOUS	K. Hang around; linger
___12. PORTLY	L. Complete agreement
___13. CORDIALLY	M. Graciously; in a friendly way
___14. EXTRAVAGANCE	N. Impressionable; easily influenced
___15. SUSCEPTIBLE	O. Being courteous with a superior air
___16. OBSCURE	P. Hateful
___17. ODIOUS	Q. Comfort; compassion
___18. MELANCHOLY	R. Avoidance
___19. LOITER	S. Humorous; merry
___20. RESOLUTE	T. Dark; vague; unclear
___21. ABSTINENCE	U. Pleads on another's behalf
___22. LATENT	V. Dormant; hidden
___23. PRODIGIOUSLY	W. Going on foot; walking
___24. RECUMBENT	X. Extremely abundant; excessive
___25. FACETIOUS	Y. Enormously; hugely

A Christmas Carol Vocabulary Matching 2 Answer Key

Q - 1. CONSOLATION
I - 2. ENCOMPASS
U - 3. INTERCEDES
B - 4. DISDAINING
F - 5. OFFICIOUS
L - 6. UNANIMITY
O - 7. CONDESCENSION
H - 8. LIVID
W - 9. PEDESTRIAN
E - 10. BENEVOLENCE
J - 11. INFAMOUS
G - 12. PORTLY
M - 13. CORDIALLY
X - 14. EXTRAVAGANCE
N - 15. SUSCEPTIBLE
T - 16. OBSCURE
P - 17. ODIOUS
D - 18. MELANCHOLY
K - 19. LOITER
A - 20. RESOLUTE
R - 21. ABSTINENCE
V - 22. LATENT
Y - 23. PRODIGIOUSLY
C - 24. RECUMBENT
S - 25. FACETIOUS

A. Determined
B. Treating with scorn or contempt
C. Reclining; lying down
D. Sadness; depression; gloom
E. Generosity; kindness
F. Meddlesome; self-important
G. Stout; fat
H. Angry; furious
I. Surround
J. Well-known for bad reasons
K. Hang around; linger
L. Complete agreement
M. Graciously; in a friendly way
N. Impressionable; easily influenced
O. Being courteous with a superior air
P. Hateful
Q. Comfort; compassion
R. Avoidance
S. Humorous; merry
T. Dark; vague; unclear
U. Pleads on another's behalf
V. Dormant; hidden
W. Going on foot; walking
X. Extremely abundant; excessive
Y. Enormously; hugely

A Christmas Carol Vocabulary Matching 3

___ 1. RESOLUTE   A. Reclining; lying down

___ 2. FETTERED   B. Determined

___ 3. SUPPLICATION   C. Hang around; linger

___ 4. INFAMOUS   D. Poor; penniless

___ 5. FEIGN   E. Shackled; chained

___ 6. PORTLY   F. Spirit

___ 7. DISPELLED   G. Threatening

___ 8. ILLUSTRIOUS   H. Scattered; caused to vanish

___ 9. INEXORABLE   I. Relentless; unyielding

___10. LATENT   J. Hateful

___11. DESTITUTE   K. Avoidance

___12. EXTRAVAGANCE   L. Softens in attitude or temper

___13. ENCOMPASS   M. Extremely abundant; excessive

___14. COVETOUS   N. Well-known for bad reasons

___15. LOITER   O. Glorious; brilliant

___16. RECUMBENT   P. Dormant; hidden

___17. LIVID   Q. Related; belonging to the same family

___18. ESSENCE   R. Very bad; offensive

___19. KINDRED   S. Graciously; in a friendly way

___20. ABSTINENCE   T. Desirous of what someone else has

___21. EXECRABLE   U. Pretend

___22. RELENTS   V. Asking for humbly or earnestly

___23. OMINOUS   W. Stout; fat

___24. CORDIALLY   X. Surround

___25. ODIOUS   Y. Angry; furious

A Christmas Carol Vocabulary Matching 3 Answer Key

B - 1. RESOLUTE   A. Reclining; lying down

E - 2. FETTERED   B. Determined

V - 3. SUPPLICATION   C. Hang around; linger

N - 4. INFAMOUS   D. Poor; penniless

U - 5. FEIGN   E. Shackled; chained

W - 6. PORTLY   F. Spirit

H - 7. DISPELLED   G. Threatening

O - 8. ILLUSTRIOUS   H. Scattered; caused to vanish

I - 9. INEXORABLE   I. Relentless; unyielding

P - 10. LATENT   J. Hateful

D - 11. DESTITUTE   K. Avoidance

M - 12. EXTRAVAGANCE   L. Softens in attitude or temper

X - 13. ENCOMPASS   M. Extremely abundant; excessive

T - 14. COVETOUS   N. Well-known for bad reasons

C - 15. LOITER   O. Glorious; brilliant

A - 16. RECUMBENT   P. Dormant; hidden

Y - 17. LIVID   Q. Related; belonging to the same family

F - 18. ESSENCE   R. Very bad; offensive

Q - 19. KINDRED   S. Graciously; in a friendly way

K - 20. ABSTINENCE   T. Desirous of what someone else has

R - 21. EXECRABLE   U. Pretend

L - 22. RELENTS   V. Asking for humbly or earnestly

G - 23. OMINOUS   W. Stout; fat

S - 24. CORDIALLY   X. Surround

J - 25. ODIOUS   Y. Angry; furious

A Christmas Carol Vocabulary Matching 4

___ 1. ALTERATION	A. Angry; furious
___ 2. MELANCHOLY	B. Hang around; linger
___ 3. FACETIOUS	C. Change
___ 4. ILLUSTRIOUS	D. Dark; vague; unclear
___ 5. INFAMOUS	E. Ill-humored; sullen
___ 6. REMONSTRATED	F. Softens in attitude or temper
___ 7. SUSCEPTIBLE	G. Glorious; brilliant
___ 8. PRECEPTS	H. Being courteous with a superior air
___ 9. UBIQUITOUS	I. Desirous of what someone else has
___10. CONSOLATION	J. Impressionable; easily influenced
___11. CONDESCENSION	K. Meddlesome; self-important
___12. OFFICIOUS	L. Comfort; compassion
___13. ADVERSARY	M. Well-known for bad reasons
___14. SORDID	N. Humorous; merry
___15. PORTLY	O. Practical rules guiding conduct
___16. DISPELLED	P. Protested
___17. BLITHE	Q. Opponent; enemy
___18. LIVID	R. Being everywhere
___19. COVETOUS	S. Filthy; vile
___20. OBSCURE	T. Sadness; depression; gloom
___21. MOROSE	U. Stout; fat
___22. RELENTS	V. Joyous; happy
___23. INEXORABLE	W. Complete agreement
___24. LOITER	X. Relentless; unyielding
___25. UNANIMITY	Y. Scattered; caused to vanish

A Christmas Carol Vocabulary Matching 4 Answer Key

C - 1. ALTERATION   A. Angry; furious

T - 2. MELANCHOLY   B. Hang around; linger

N - 3. FACETIOUS   C. Change

G - 4. ILLUSTRIOUS   D. Dark; vague; unclear

M - 5. INFAMOUS   E. Ill-humored; sullen

P - 6. REMONSTRATED   F. Softens in attitude or temper

J - 7. SUSCEPTIBLE   G. Glorious; brilliant

O - 8. PRECEPTS   H. Being courteous with a superior air

R - 9. UBIQUITOUS   I. Desirous of what someone else has

L - 10. CONSOLATION   J. Impressionable; easily influenced

H -11. CONDESCENSION   K. Meddlesome; self-important

K -12. OFFICIOUS   L. Comfort; compassion

Q -13. ADVERSARY   M. Well-known for bad reasons

S -14. SORDID   N. Humorous; merry

U -15. PORTLY   O. Practical rules guiding conduct

Y -16. DISPELLED   P. Protested

V -17. BLITHE   Q. Opponent; enemy

A -18. LIVID   R. Being everywhere

I - 19. COVETOUS   S. Filthy; vile

D -20. OBSCURE   T. Sadness; depression; gloom

E -21. MOROSE   U. Stout; fat

F -22. RELENTS   V. Joyous; happy

X -23. INEXORABLE   W. Complete agreement

B -24. LOITER   X. Relentless; unyielding

W -25. UNANIMITY   Y. Scattered; caused to vanish

A Christmas Carol Vocabulary Magic Squares 1

Match the definition with the vocabulary word. Put your answers in the magic squares below. When your answers are correct, all columns and rows will add to the same number.

A. SUSCEPTIBLE   G. PORTLY   M. RECOMPENSED
B. PEDESTRIAN   H. RESOLUTE   N. LOITER
C. ODIOUS   I. PRECEPTS   O. PRODIGIOUSLY
D. DISDAINING   J. RECUMBENT   P. BLITHE
E. FETTERED   K. ESSENCE
F. REMONSTRATED   L. OBSCURE

1. Hateful   9. Repaid

2. Reclining; lying down   10. Determined

3. Protested   11. Dark; vague; unclear

4. Enormously; hugely   12. Impressionable; easily influenced

5. Joyous; happy   13. Going on foot; walking

6. Shackled; chained   14. Spirit

7. Practical rules guiding conduct 15. Stout; fat

8. Treating with scorn or contempt 16. Hang around; linger

A=	B=	C=	D=
E=	F=	G=	H=
I=	J=	K=	L=
M=	N=	O=	P=

A Christmas Carol Vocabulary Magic Squares 1 Answer Key

Match the definition with the vocabulary word. Put your answers in the magic squares below. When your answers are correct, all columns and rows will add to the same number.

A. SUSCEPTIBLE   G. PORTLY   M. RECOMPENSED
B. PEDESTRIAN   H. RESOLUTE   N. LOITER
C. ODIOUS   I. PRECEPTS   O. PRODIGIOUSLY
D. DISDAINING   J. RECUMBENT   P. BLITHE
E. FETTERED   K. ESSENCE
F. REMONSTRATED   L. OBSCURE

1. Hateful

2. Reclining; lying down

3. Protested

4. Enormously; hugely

5. Joyous; happy

6. Shackled; chained

7. Practical rules guiding conduct

8. Treating with scorn or contempt

9. Repaid

10. Determined

11. Dark; vague; unclear

12. Impressionable; easily influenced

13. Going on foot; walking

14. Spirit

15. Stout; fat

16. Hang around; linger

A=12	B=13	C=1	D=8
E=6	F=3	G=15	H=10
I=7	J=2	K=14	L=11
M=9	N=16	O=4	P=5

A Christmas Carol Vocabulary Magic Squares 2

Match the definition with the vocabulary word. Put your answers in the magic squares below. When your answers are correct, all columns and rows will add to the same number.

A. FACETIOUS   G. ALTERATION   M. ILLUSTRIOUS
B. REMONSTRATED   H. AGITATED   N. CONSOLATION
C. MOROSE   I. FETTERED   O. PEDESTRIAN
D. SUPPLICATION   J. LATENT   P. EXECRABLE
E. KINDRED   K. OBSCURE
F. COVETOUS   L. RESOLUTE

1. Going on foot; walking

2. Dormant; hidden

3. Stirred up; disturbed

4. Humorous; merry

5. Asking for humbly or earnestly

6. Related; belonging to the same family

7. Dark; vague; unclear

8. Comfort; compassion

9. Desirous of what someone else has

10. Ill-humored; sullen

11. Glorious; brilliant

12. Determined

13. Shackled; chained

14. Very bad; offensive

15. Protested

16. Change

A=	B=	C=	D=
E=	F=	G=	H=
I=	J=	K=	L=
M=	N=	O=	P=

A Christmas Carol Vocabulary Magic Squares 2 Answer Key

Match the definition with the vocabulary word. Put your answers in the magic squares below. When your answers are correct, all columns and rows will add to the same number.

A. FACETIOUS
B. REMONSTRATED
C. MOROSE
D. SUPPLICATION
E. KINDRED
F. COVETOUS

G. ALTERATION
H. AGITATED
I. FETTERED
J. LATENT
K. OBSCURE
L. RESOLUTE

M. ILLUSTRIOUS
N. CONSOLATION
O. PEDESTRIAN
P. EXECRABLE

1. Going on foot; walking

2. Dormant; hidden

3. Stirred up; disturbed

4. Humorous; merry

5. Asking for humbly or earnestly

6. Related; belonging to the same family

7. Dark; vague; unclear

8. Comfort; compassion

9. Desirous of what someone else has

10. Ill-humored; sullen

11. Glorious; brilliant

12. Determined

13. Shackled; chained

14. Very bad; offensive

15. Protested

16. Change

A=4	B=15	C=10	D=5
E=6	F=9	G=16	H=3
I=13	J=2	K=7	L=12
M=11	N=8	O=1	P=14

A Christmas Carol Vocabulary Magic Squares 3

Match the definition with the vocabulary word. Put your answers in the magic squares below. When your answers are correct, all columns and rows will add to the same number.

A. ODIOUS
B. RECOMPENSED
C. CONSOLATION
D. BLITHE
E. CORDIALLY
F. COVETOUS

G. INEXORABLE
H. SUPPLICATION
I. FACETIOUS
J. ENCOMPASS
K. DESTITUTE
L. KINDRED

M. PEDESTRIAN
N. FEIGN
O. INFAMOUS
P. UBIQUITOUS

1. Asking for humbly or earnestly

2. Going on foot; walking

3. Repaid

4. Poor; penniless

5. Surround

6. Comfort; compassion

7. Being everywhere

8. Graciously; in a friendly way

9. Well-known for bad reasons

10. Desirous of what someone else has

11. Humorous; merry

12. Joyous; happy

13. Hateful

14. Related; belonging to the same family

15. Relentless; unyielding

16. Pretend

A=	B=	C=	D=
E=	F=	G=	H=
I=	J=	K=	L=
M=	N=	O=	P=

A Christmas Carol Vocabulary Magic Squares 3 Answer Key

Match the definition with the vocabulary word. Put your answers in the magic squares below. When your answers are correct, all columns and rows will add to the same number.

A. ODIOUS   G. INEXORABLE   M. PEDESTRIAN
B. RECOMPENSED   H. SUPPLICATION   N. FEIGN
C. CONSOLATION   I. FACETIOUS   O. INFAMOUS
D. BLITHE   J. ENCOMPASS   P. UBIQUITOUS
E. CORDIALLY   K. DESTITUTE
F. COVETOUS   L. KINDRED

1. Asking for humbly or earnestly

2. Going on foot; walking

3. Repaid

4. Poor; penniless

5. Surround

6. Comfort; compassion

7. Being everywhere

8. Graciously; in a friendly way

9. Well-known for bad reasons

10. Desirous of what someone else has

11. Humorous; merry

12. Joyous; happy

13. Hateful

14. Related; belonging to the same family

15. Relentless; unyielding

16. Pretend

A=13	B=3	C=6	D=12
E=8	F=10	G=15	H=1
I=11	J=5	K=4	L=14
M=2	N=16	O=9	P=7

A Christmas Carol Vocabulary Magic Squares 4

Match the definition with the vocabulary word. Put your answers in the magic squares below. When your answers are correct, all columns and rows will add to the same number.

A. EXTRAVAGANCE   G. EXECRABLE   M. OBSCURE
B. ADVERSARY   H. PEDESTRIAN   N. OMINOUS
C. SUPPLICATION   I. LOITER   O. MOROSE
D. ABSTINENCE   J. CONDESCENSION P. LATENT
E. RESOLUTE   K. FEIGN
F. RECUMBENT   L. PORTLY

1. Reclining; lying down

2. Hang around; linger

3. Ill-humored; sullen

4. Avoidance

5. Dark; vague; unclear

6. Opponent; enemy

7. Going on foot; walking

8. Pretend

9. Asking for humbly or earnestly

10. Dormant; hidden

11. Being courteous with a superior air

12. Determined

13. Stout; fat

14. Very bad; offensive

15. Extremely abundant; excessive

16. Threatening

A=	B=	C=	D=
E=	F=	G=	H=
I=	J=	K=	L=
M=	N=	O=	P=

A Christmas Carol Vocabulary Magic Squares 4 Answer Key

Match the definition with the vocabulary word. Put your answers in the magic squares below. When your answers are correct, all columns and rows will add to the same number.

A. EXTRAVAGANCE   G. EXECRABLE   M. OBSCURE
B. ADVERSARY   H. PEDESTRIAN   N. OMINOUS
C. SUPPLICATION   I. LOITER   O. MOROSE
D. ABSTINENCE   J. CONDESCENSION P. LATENT
E. RESOLUTE   K. FEIGN
F. RECUMBENT   L. PORTLY

1. Reclining; lying down

2. Hang around; linger

3. Ill-humored; sullen

4. Avoidance

5. Dark; vague; unclear

6. Opponent; enemy

7. Going on foot; walking

8. Pretend

9. Asking for humbly or earnestly

10. Dormant; hidden

11. Being courteous with a superior air

12. Determined

13. Stout; fat

14. Very bad; offensive

15. Extremely abundant; excessive

16. Threatening

A=15	B=6	C=9	D=4
E=12	F=1	G=14	H=7
I=2	J=11	K=8	L=13
M=5	N=16	O=3	P=10

A Christmas Carol Vocabulary Word Search 1

```
K  C  N  A  I  R  T  S  E  D  E  P  A  G  I  T  A  T  E  D
I  S  O  D  S  R  T  B  N  H  N  R  L  M  M  R  F  L  N  F
N  S  W  V  F  G  L  H  T  L  G  E  T  E  N  H  E  P  Y  N
D  A  G  E  E  O  D  I  O  U  S  C  E  L  O  I  T  E  R  Q
R  P  D  R  F  T  L  S  S  R  O  E  R  A  I  R  T  I  D  W
E  M  L  S  Z  B  O  U  V  N  N  P  A  N  T  E  E  L  I  R
D  O  B  A  H  G  O  U  S  F  E  T  T  C  A  C  R  L  S  W
I  C  S  R  Z  I  S  O  S  C  S  S  I  H  C  O  E  U  P  T
H  N  L  Y  T  B  L  V  N  R  U  H  O  O  I  M  D  S  E  L
C  E  F  E  N  A  V  E  K  S  O  F  N  L  L  P  I  T  L  Q
S  O  C  A  T  H  L  F  C  Q  I  X  K  Y  P  E  N  R  L  L
T  A  N  I  M  O  Z  E  R  U  C  S  B  O  P  N  E  I  E  Z
F  W  O  D  V  O  P  J  X  Q  A  Q  Z  K  U  S  X  O  D  S
T  N  R  E  E  T  U  M  N  G  P  Z  Z  D  S  E  O  U  V  V
N  C  N  W  I  S  V  S  X  B  A  M  E  F  P  D  R  S  T  L
E  E  O  B  I  K  C  G  O  W  C  T  F  E  O  P  A  G  H  L
B  D  L  R  V  N  N  E  K  F  A  N  Y  I  R  X  B  T  M  X
M  E  E  E  D  T  T  M  N  R  F  T  G  G  T  B  L  W  E  F
U  N  S  S  K  I  T  E  T  S  I  I  W  N  L  B  E  T  O  L
C  C  T  S  T  V  A  S  R  M  I  S  C  T  Y  M  U  C  M  L
E  G  N  E  M  I  N  L  I  C  O  O  N  I  O  L  F  G  I  R
R  J  E  N  C  O  T  N  L  R  E  E  N  R  O  B  W  V  N  F
M  V  L  C  M  C  A  U  D  Y  T  D  O  S  N  U  I  B  O  J
Q  K  E  E  H  N  O  I  T  A  T  S  E  T  E  D  S  J  U  C
G  K  R  C  U  S  D  J  L  E  E  R  H  S  C  J  W  W  S  X
```

Angry; furious (5)
Asking for humbly or earnestly (12)
Being courteous with a superior air (13)
Change (10)
Comfort; compassion (11)
Complete agreement (9)
Dark; vague; unclear (7)
Desirous of what someone else has (8)
Determined (8)
Dormant; hidden (6)
Filthy; vile (6)
Generosity; kindness (11)
Glorious; brilliant (11)
Going on foot; walking (10)
Graciously; in a friendly way (9)
Hang around; linger (6)
Hateful (6)
Humorous; merry (9)
Ill-humored; sullen (6)
Impressionable; easily influenced (11)
Intense dislike (11)
Joyous; happy (6)
Meddlesome; self-important (9)

Opponent; enemy (9)
Pleads on another's behalf (10)
Poor; penniless (9)
Practical rules guiding conduct (8)
Pretend (5)
Protested (12)
Reclining; lying down (9)
Related; belonging to the same family (7)
Relentless; unyielding (10)
Repaid (11)
Sadness; depression; gloom (10)
Scattered; caused to vanish (9)
Shackled; chained (8)
Softens in attitude or temper (7)
Spacious; large (9)
Spirit (7)
Stirred up; disturbed (8)
Stout; fat (6)
Surround (9)
Threatening (7)
Well-known for bad reasons (8)

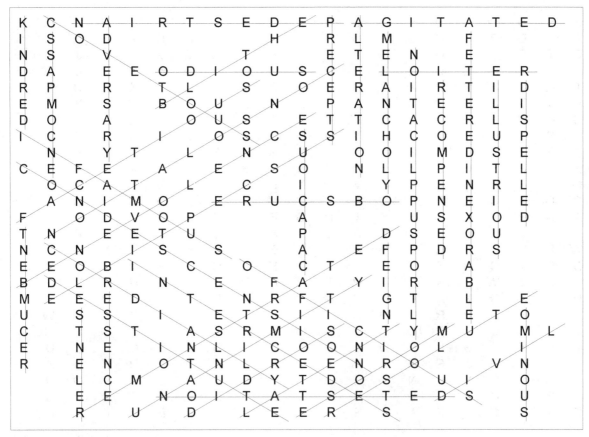

Angry; furious (5)
Asking for humbly or earnestly (12)
Being courteous with a superior air (13)
Change (10)
Comfort; compassion (11)
Complete agreement (9)
Dark; vague; unclear (7)
Desirous of what someone else has (8)
Determined (8)
Dormant; hidden (6)
Filthy; vile (6)
Generosity; kindness (11)
Glorious; brilliant (11)
Going on foot; walking (10)
Graciously; in a friendly way (9)
Hang around; linger (6)
Hateful (6)
Humorous; merry (9)
Ill-humored; sullen (6)
Impressionable; easily influenced (11)
Intense dislike (11)
Joyous; happy (6)
Meddlesome; self-important (9)

Opponent; enemy (9)
Pleads on another's behalf (10)
Poor; penniless (9)
Practical rules guiding conduct (8)
Pretend (5)
Protested (12)
Reclining; lying down (9)
Related; belonging to the same family (7)
Relentless; unyielding (10)
Repaid (11)
Sadness; depression; gloom (10)
Scattered; caused to vanish (9)
Shackled; chained (8)
Softens in attitude or temper (7)
Spacious; large (9)
Spirit (7)
Stirred up; disturbed (8)
Stout; fat (6)
Surround (9)
Threatening (7)
Well-known for bad reasons (8)

A Christmas Carol Vocabulary Word Search 2

```
F  B  D  W  Y  W  K  J  U  S  N  U  S  U  O  T  E  V  O  C
A  Y  E  R  U  C  S  B  O  B  L  J  N  L  P  D  T  T  Q  Q
C  T  S  Y  J  G  J  D  R  C  I  R  K  A  Q  J  I  S  J  X
E  S  T  P  E  C  E  R  P  H  T  Q  N  V  N  N  D  O  M  Q
T  Q  I  T  D  R  X  Q  D  E  C  A  U  O  X  I  K  R  U  X
I  V  T  E  E  Y  S  D  L  P  I  C  I  I  V  R  M  D  Y  S
O  C  U  T  X  J  E  B  F  R  K  T  B  I  T  K  H  I  L  G
U  S  T  N  E  T  A  L  T  H  A  E  L  N  Z  O  B  D  T  C
S  E  E  Y  A  R  R  S  T  L  N  B  O  F  D  L  U  B  R  Y
F  C  R  T  O  S  E  A  O  E  N  I  S  B  I  X  V  S  O  J
M  K  I  X  D  D  S  S  V  M  T  L  N  T  Y  B  N  C  P  S
C  G  E  C  E  T  N  O  A  A  J  M  H  L  I  D  G  W  C  L
A  N  W  P  N  O  L  Y  T  D  G  E  L  T  E  N  I  M  A  C
I  J  V  E  C  E  W  S  B  S  V  A  S  S  J  K  E  Z  P  Z
W  F  L  T  N  N  E  Y  E  A  I  E  N  S  R  S  F  N  A  Y
D  E  J  C  N  T  G  L  L  D  P  E  R  C  E  R  D  T  C  C
R  I  E  W  E  K  B  T  R  T  P  L  T  S  E  N  N  J  I  E
N  T  S  D  X  A  E  O  N  M  W  G  O  S  A  E  C  R  O  S
L  F  Z  D  R  R  C  G  O  S  T  R  O  I  B  R  D  E  U  W
Q  B  S  C  A  R  Q  C  U  B  O  L  L  M  T  E  Y  O  S  M
V  R  E  T  S  I  E  O  Z  M  U  V  U  D  R  E  M  J  Z  D
P  X  I  D  J  R  N  B  M  T  Y  C  X  D  N  A  R  H  B  X
E  O  P  P  Y  I  N  I  E  M  E  Y  N  D  F  D  S  K  Q  D
N  R  Z  B  M  B  D  J  N  R  B  I  Q  N  W  G  T  D  W  C
E  N  C  O  M  P  A  S  S  G  K  D  I  S  P  E  L  L  E  D
```

Angry; furious (5)
Avoidance (10)
Being everywhere (10)
Change (10)
Comfort; compassion (11)
Complete agreement (9)
Dark; vague; unclear (7)
Desirous of what someone else has (8)
Determined (8)
Dormant; hidden (6)
Extremely abundant; excessive (12)
Filthy; vile (6)
Generosity; kindness (11)
Going on foot; walking (10)
Graciously; in a friendly way (9)
Hang around; linger (6)
Hateful (6)
Humorous; merry (9)
Ill-humored; sullen (6)
Intense dislike (11)
Joyous; happy (6)
Opponent; enemy (9)
Poor; penniless (9)

Practical rules guiding conduct (8)
Pretend (5)
Reclining; lying down (9)
Related; belonging to the same family (7)
Relentless; unyielding (10)
Repaid (11)
Scattered; caused to vanish (9)
Shackled; chained (8)
Softens in attitude or temper (7)
Spacious; large (9)
Spirit (7)
Stirred up; disturbed (8)
Stout; fat (6)
Surround (9)
Threatening (7)
Treating with scorn or contempt (10)
Very bad; offensive (9)
Well-known for bad reasons (8)

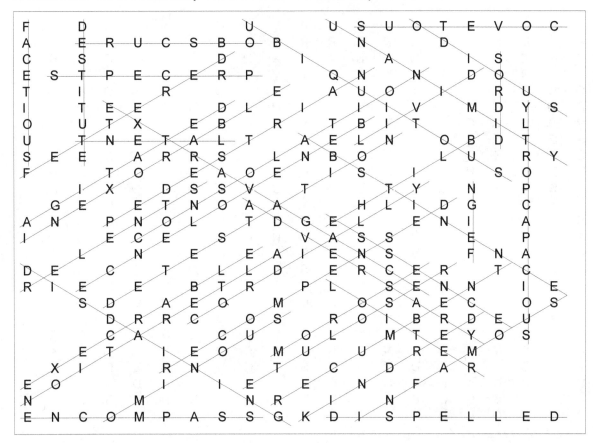

Angry; furious (5)
Avoidance (10)
Being everywhere (10)
Change (10)
Comfort; compassion (11)
Complete agreement (9)
Dark; vague; unclear (7)
Desirous of what someone else has (8)
Determined (8)
Dormant; hidden (6)
Extremely abundant; excessive (12)
Filthy; vile (6)
Generosity; kindness (11)
Going on foot; walking (10)
Graciously; in a friendly way (9)
Hang around; linger (6)
Hateful (6)
Humorous; merry (9)
Ill-humored; sullen (6)
Intense dislike (11)
Joyous; happy (6)
Opponent; enemy (9)
Poor; penniless (9)

Practical rules guiding conduct (8)
Pretend (5)
Reclining; lying down (9)
Related; belonging to the same family (7)
Relentless; unyielding (10)
Repaid (11)
Scattered; caused to vanish (9)
Shackled; chained (8)
Softens in attitude or temper (7)
Spacious; large (9)
Spirit (7)
Stirred up; disturbed (8)
Stout; fat (6)
Surround (9)
Threatening (7)
Treating with scorn or contempt (10)
Very bad; offensive (9)
Well-known for bad reasons (8)

A Christmas Carol Vocabulary Word Search 3

```
K B G B W I Y L V U B I Q U I T O U S G
F I L B C P N N O R P Y P Y P B B U O T
Q G N I H G G T D I D X Q R S D S D R B
S V R D T T X S E L T V L C E C D G D Y
O H Z T R H J U F R J E U G E C M D I M
P M W K T E E P E Z C R R P N O E D D E
R D I W G R D P I K E E T L P N E P C X
A E P N C N M L G F Y I D R F S R N T T
D T L X O A L I N L B T O E T O E E N S
V E F E H U P C L L Q D R I S L C X E D
E S B K N Q S A E G I S T S O A O E B R
R T M L L T I T C G Y U S V I T M C M T
S A Y O X D S I I I T U E L N I P R U K
A T W G R S P O P E O N L M E O E A C M
R I M O U O U N D I E U D E X N N B E P
Y O C O R S S E T B S I S L O A S L R K
Q N I T L D R E Y T V A F A R I E E C D
Q D L Y H E C S R I Q G N N A R D N O D
O Y G F T A J I L N L I B C B T P C V L
X X S T F C O K L L D T F H L S F O E R
B R E M N U L N T H A A D O E E Y M T K
V F C Y S Y D Y M C B T H L T D Z P O K
D I S D A I N I N G Z E E Y S E D A U V
G R G D I S P E L L E D T N K P Z S S X
R E S O L U T E S S E N C E T D S S F Q
```

ADVERSARY   DISPELLED   LATENT   PRODIGIOUSLY

AGITATED   ENCOMPASS   LIVID   RECOMPENSED

BENEVOLENCE   ESSENCE   LOITER   RECUMBENT

BLITHE   EXECRABLE   MELANCHOLY   RELENTS

CAPACIOUS   FACETIOUS   MOROSE   RESOLUTE

CONSOLATION   FEIGN   OBSCURE   SORDID

CORDIALLY   FETTERED   ODIOUS   SUPPLICATION

COVETOUS   ILLUSTRIOUS   OMINOUS   SUSCEPTIBLE

DESTITUTE   INEXORABLE   PEDESTRIAN   UBIQUITOUS

DETESTATION   INTERCEDES   PORTLY

DISDAINING   KINDRED   PRECEPTS

ADVERSARY	DISPELLED	LATENT	PRODIGIOUSLY
AGITATED	ENCOMPASS	LIVID	RECOMPENSED
BENEVOLENCE	ESSENCE	LOITER	RECUMBENT
BLITHE	EXECRABLE	MELANCHOLY	RELENTS
CAPACIOUS	FACETIOUS	MOROSE	RESOLUTE
CONSOLATION	FEIGN	OBSCURE	SORDID
CORDIALLY	FETTERED	ODIOUS	SUPPLICATION
COVETOUS	ILLUSTRIOUS	OMINOUS	SUSCEPTIBLE
DESTITUTE	INEXORABLE	PEDESTRIAN	UBIQUITOUS
DETESTATION	INTERCEDES	PORTLY	
DISDAINING	KINDRED	PRECEPTS	

```
Y  D  E  R  E  T  T  E  F  B  P  G  B  S  B  R  Y  F  T  Q
F  A  C  E  T  I  O  U  S  K  K  E  U  S  P  E  X  N  J  Q
S  U  O  M  A  F  N  I  R  V  P  O  D  V  J  L  Q  P  C  G
F  Y  T  O  Y  R  M  N  C  W  I  R  B  E  T  E  M  Y  O  V
R  X  Z  N  R  L  V  D  T  C  O  D  W  U  S  N  L  D  N  L
H  Q  P  S  A  G  I  T  A  T  E  D  B  L  I  T  H  E  S  T
V  T  T  T  S  H  V  P  J  R  I  I  I  Z  R  S  R  S  O  B
W  H  E  R  R  L  A  N  D  D  Q  V  R  O  S  B  A  I  L  Q
Q  N  I  A  E  C  C  N  R  U  E  I  P  E  U  P  L  N  A  Z
T  W  L  T  V  T  I  O  I  C  N  L  T  P  M  S  O  E  T  N
C  J  L  E  D  K  S  T  N  V  E  U  B  O  B  E  I  X  I  P
O  J  U  D  A  P  O  E  Q  D  T  X  C  K  R  S  T  O  O  Y
R  D  S  O  I  U  S  V  P  I  E  N  E  U  H  S  E  R  N  S
D  C  T  F  S  S  R  Z  T  R  E  S  C  C  U  J  R  A  M  G
I  O  R  F  E  H  D  S  F  C  E  S  C  O  R  E  W  B  O  K
A  V  I  I  C  U  E  A  E  M  B  C  N  E  T  A  N  L  R  F
L  E  O  C  N  D  N  Y  I  O  E  I  E  U  N  W  B  E  O  R
L  T  U  I  E  T  I  A  G  N  M  L  L  P  X  S  K  L  S  L
Y  O  S  O  N  G  E  S  N  O  I  O  A  G  T  L  I  S  E  J
P  U  D  U  I  M  F  R  P  I  S  N  F  N  N  S  M  O  M  T
H  S  M  S  T  N  L  M  C  E  M  Y  G  G  C  D  T  R  N  B
W  H  N  Y  S  D  L  R  R  E  L  I  D  G  S  H  D  B  L  D
F  T  N  E  B  M  U  C  E  R  D  L  T  V  Y  H  O  K  S  L
N  O  I  T  A  T  S  E  T  E  D  E  E  Y  W  T  K  L  W  S
P  R  O  D  I  G  I  O  U  S  L  Y  S  D  F  Q  F  Z  Y  Z
```

ABSTINENCE	DISDAINING	INTERCEDES	PEDESTRIAN
ADVERSARY	DISPELLED	KINDRED	PORTLY
AGITATED	ENCOMPASS	LATENT	PRECEPTS
BLITHE	ESSENCE	LIVID	PRODIGIOUSLY
CAPACIOUS	EXECRABLE	LOITER	RECUMBENT
CONDESCENSION	FACETIOUS	MELANCHOLY	RELENTS
CONSOLATION	FEIGN	MOROSE	REMONSTRATED
CORDIALLY	FETTERED	OBSCURE	RESOLUTE
COVETOUS	ILLUSTRIOUS	ODIOUS	SORDID
DESTITUTE	INEXORABLE	OFFICIOUS	UBIQUITOUS
DETESTATION	INFAMOUS	OMINOUS	UNANIMITY

A Christmas Carol Vocabulary Word Search 4 Answer Key

```
    D E R E T T E F       P       S       R
  F A C E T I O U S       E U           R E L
  S U O M A F N I         O D         E     C
        M A Y           I       U S N   L   O
      O R   L       C O D     U       H E Y N
    E N S   A G I T A T E D B L I T H E   S S
      S R   P     R I I I     R   R   A   O O
    E T R   A   D D Q V   O       P L   R   L
  N I A E   C C N R U E I P E U   S A I N   A
T C L T   K S T N I C   T X C     E L O X   T
C O L E D A O E   E   D T U C   R   O T N   I
R V U O I U S   P I E N E U S U   S E R O   O
D E S F S S   D S F T R E C C U R   E I A M N
I T T O   U E A   M B C N E T A   B R A B O
A O R F U D N I   O E I E U N   A   S   L R
L U I I C   E I M L L P T   B   S   L   E O
L S O C N T I G N O O L A N   S   O     L S
Y   U I E S   P I N M I A N   N     H   Y E
    S O N R   C E M O S N G   C     O     N
      U S T     R L I         H       L   N
    T N E B M U C E R D L T       O     Y
  N O I T A T S E T E D E E Y       L
  P R O D I G I O U S L Y S D
```

ABSTINENCE   DISDAINING   INTERCEDES   PEDESTRIAN

ADVERSARY   DISPELLED   KINDRED   PORTLY

AGITATED   ENCOMPASS   LATENT   PRECEPTS

BLITHE   ESSENCE   LIVID   PRODIGIOUSLY

CAPACIOUS   EXECRABLE   LOITER   RECUMBENT

CONDESCENSION   FACETIOUS   MELANCHOLY   RELENTS

CONSOLATION   FEIGN   MOROSE   REMONSTRATED

CORDIALLY   FETTERED   OBSCURE   RESOLUTE

COVETOUS   ILLUSTRIOUS   ODIOUS   SORDID

DESTITUTE   INEXORABLE   OFFICIOUS   UBIQUITOUS

DETESTATION   INFAMOUS   OMINOUS   UNANIMITY

A Christmas Carol Vocabulary Crossword 1

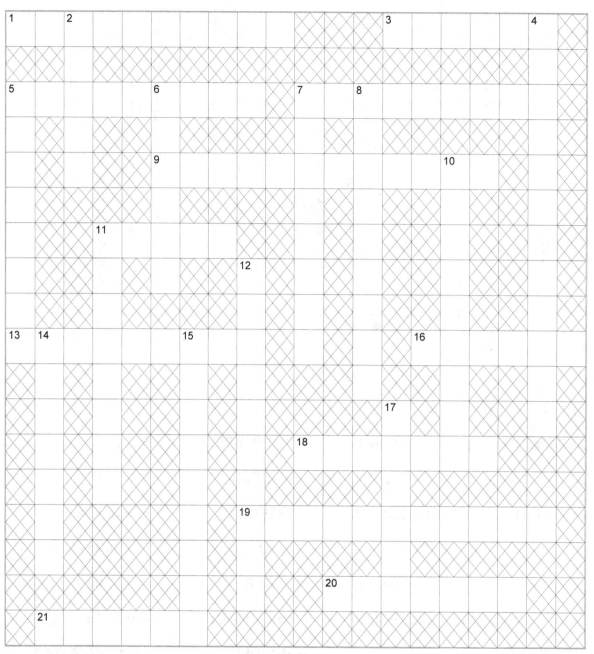

Across
1. Sadness; depression; gloom
3. Joyous; happy
5. Opponent; enemy
7. Reclining; lying down
9. Protested
11. Pretend
13. Poor; penniless
16. Dormant; hidden
18. Related; belonging to the same family
19. Generosity; kindness
20. Dark; vague; unclear
21. Stout; fat

Down
2. Angry; furious
4. Extremely abundant; excessive
5. Stirred up; disturbed
6. Filthy; vile
7. Determined
8. Graciously; in a friendly way
10. Very bad; offensive
11. Shackled; chained
12. Relentless; unyielding
14. Spirit
15. Complete agreement
17. Hateful

A Christmas Carol Vocabulary Crossword 1 Answer Key

¹M	²E	L	A	N	C	H	O	L	Y			³B	L	I	T	H	⁴E
	I															X
⁵A	D	V	E	R	⁶S	A	R	Y		⁷R	E	⁸C	U	M	B	E	N	T
G	I				O					E		O				R
I	D			⁹R	E	M	O	N	S	T	R	A	T	¹⁰E	D	A
A				D				O	D			X		V
A		¹¹F	E	I	G	N		L	I			E		A
T		E	D		¹²I	U	A			C		G
E		T			N	T	L			R		A
¹³D	¹⁴E	S	T	I	T	U	¹⁵T	E		E	L		¹⁶L	A	T	E	N	T
	S	S		E	N	X			Y		B	C
	S	R		A	O		¹⁷O	L	E
	E	E		N	R	¹⁸K	I	N	D	R	E	D
	N	D		I	A		I
	C		¹⁹M	B	E	N	E	V	O	L	E	N	C	E
	E		I	L		U
			T	E	²⁰O	B	S	C	U	R	E
²¹P	O	R	T	L	Y

Across
1. Sadness; depression; gloom
3. Joyous; happy
5. Opponent; enemy
7. Reclining; lying down
9. Protested
11. Pretend
13. Poor; penniless
16. Dormant; hidden
18. Related; belonging to the same family
19. Generosity; kindness
20. Dark; vague; unclear
21. Stout; fat

Down
2. Angry; furious
4. Extremely abundant; excessive
5. Stirred up; disturbed
6. Filthy; vile
7. Determined
8. Graciously; in a friendly way
10. Very bad; offensive
11. Shackled; chained
12. Relentless; unyielding
14. Spirit
15. Complete agreement
17. Hateful

A Christmas Carol Vocabulary Crossword 2

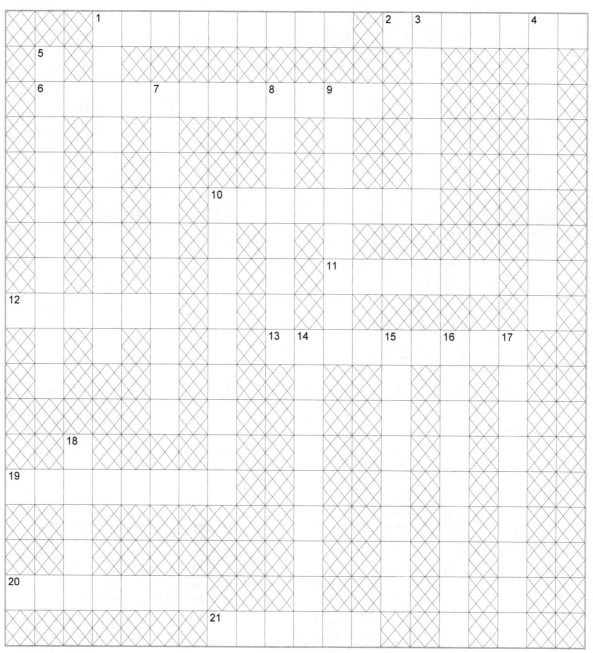

Across
1. Opponent; enemy
2. Spirit
6. Extremely abundant; excessive
10. Shackled; chained
11. Hateful
12. Ill-humored; sullen
13. Poor; penniless
19. Practical rules guiding conduct
20. Related; belonging to the same family
21. Dormant; hidden

Down
1. Change

3. Filthy; vile
4. Graciously; in a friendly way
5. Sadness; depression; gloom
7. Avoidance
8. Stirred up; disturbed
9. Desirous of what someone else has
10. Humorous; merry
14. Very bad; offensive
15. Well-known for bad reasons
16. Complete agreement
17. Surround
18. Pretend

A Christmas Carol Vocabulary Crossword 2 Answer Key

1	2	3	4	5	6	7	8	9	10	11	12	13	14	15	16	17	18	19	20
			A	D	V	E	R	S	A	R	Y		E	S	S	E	N	C	E
	M		L											O				O	
	E	X	T	R	A	V	A	G	A	N	C	E		R				R	
	L		E		B				G		O			D				D	
	A		R		S				I		V			I				I	
	N		A		T		F	E	T	T	E	R	E	D				A	
	C		T		I		A		A		T							L	
	H		I		N		C		T		O	D	I	O	U	S		L	
M	O	R	O	S	E		E		E		U							Y	
	L		N		N		T		D	E	S	T	I	T	U	T	E		
	Y				C		I			X			N		N		N		
					E		O			E			F		A		C		
		F					U			C			A		N		O		
P	R	E	C	E	P	T	S			R			M		I		M		
		I								A			O		M		P		
		G								B			U		I		A		
K	I	N	D	R	E	D				L			S		T		S		
							L	A	T	E	N	T			Y		S		

Across
1. Opponent; enemy
2. Spirit
6. Extremely abundant; excessive
10. Shackled; chained
11. Hateful
12. Ill-humored; sullen
13. Poor; penniless
19. Practical rules guiding conduct
20. Related; belonging to the same family
21. Dormant; hidden

Down
1. Change
3. Filthy; vile
4. Graciously; in a friendly way
5. Sadness; depression; gloom
7. Avoidance
8. Stirred up; disturbed
9. Desirous of what someone else has
10. Humorous; merry
14. Very bad; offensive
15. Well-known for bad reasons
16. Complete agreement
17. Surround
18. Pretend

A Christmas Carol Vocabulary Crossword 3

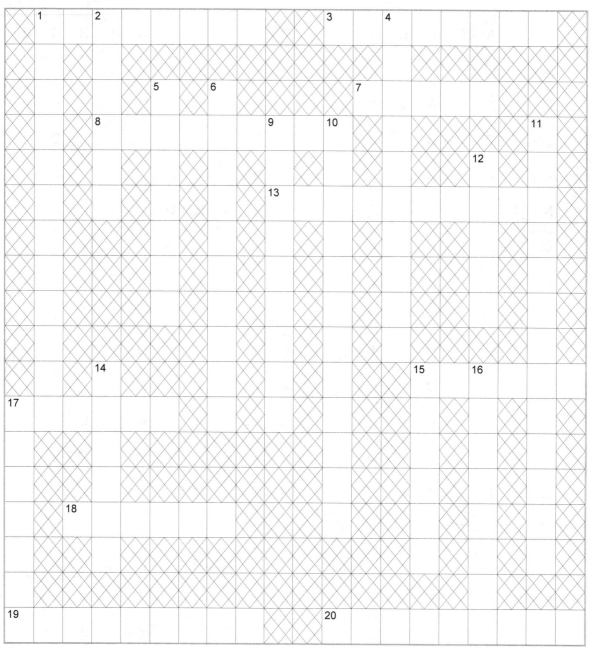

Across
1. Determined
3. Stirred up; disturbed
7. Pretend
8. Poor; penniless
13. Change
15. Hang around; linger
17. Hateful
18. Joyous; happy
19. Very bad; offensive
20. Opponent; enemy

Down
1. Protested

2. Filthy; vile
4. Relentless; unyielding
5. Spirit
6. Treating with scorn or contempt
9. Complete agreement
10. Extremely abundant; excessive
11. Being courteous with a superior air
12. Angry; furious
14. Stout; fat
15. Dormant; hidden
16. Well-known for bad reasons
17. Dark; vague; unclear

A Christmas Carol Vocabulary Crossword 3 Answer Key

Grid (Answer Key):

- 1 Across: R E S O L U T E
- 3 Across: A G I T A T E D
- 7 Across: F E I G N
- 8 Across: D E S T I T U T E
- 13 Across: A L T E R A T I O N
- 15 Across: L O I T E R
- 17 Across: O D I O U S
- 18 Across: B L I T H E
- 19 Across: E X E C R A B L E
- 20 Across: A D V E R S A R Y

- Down 1: R E M O N S T R A T E
- Down 2: S O R D I D
- Down 4: I N A N I M A T E
- Down 5: R E S E N T M E N T
- Down 6: D I S D A I N I N G
- Down 9: U N A N I M I T Y
- Down 10: E X O R B I T A N T
- Down 11: C O N D E S C E N S I O N
- Down 12: L I V I D
- Down 14: P R T Y
- Down 15: L A T E N T
- Down 16: I N F A M O U S
- Down 17: O B S C U R E

Across

1. Determined
3. Stirred up; disturbed
7. Pretend
8. Poor; penniless
13. Change
15. Hang around; linger
17. Hateful
18. Joyous; happy
19. Very bad; offensive
20. Opponent; enemy

Down

1. Protested

2. Filthy; vile
4. Relentless; unyielding
5. Spirit
6. Treating with scorn or contempt
9. Complete agreement
10. Extremely abundant; excessive
11. Being courteous with a superior air
12. Angry; furious
14. Stout; fat
15. Dormant; hidden
16. Well-known for bad reasons
17. Dark; vague; unclear

A Christmas Carol Vocabulary Crossword 4

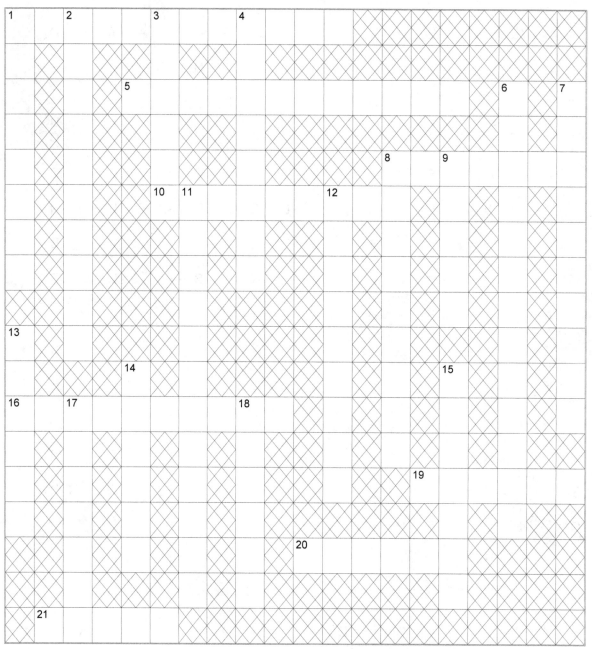

Across
1. Protested
5. Enormously; hugely
8. Softens in attitude or temper
10. Poor; penniless
16. Relentless; unyielding
19. Hateful
20. Ill-humored; sullen
21. Pretend

Down
1. Determined
2. Sadness; depression; gloom
3. Filthy; vile

4. Stirred up; disturbed
6. Being courteous with a superior air
7. Treating with scorn or contempt
8. Reclining; lying down
9. Angry; furious
11. Extremely abundant; excessive
12. Complete agreement
13. Joyous; happy
14. Stout; fat
15. Related; belonging to the same family
17. Spirit
18. Hang around; linger

A Christmas Carol Vocabulary Crossword 4 Answer Key

¹R	²E	M	O	³N	S	T	⁴R	A	T	E	D				
E	E			O			G								
S	L	⁵P	R	O	D	I	G	I	O	U	S	L	Y	⁶C		⁷D
O	A	D		T			A							O		I
L	N	I				A			⁸R	⁹E	L	E	N	T	S
U	C	¹⁰D	¹¹E	S	T	I	¹²T	U	T	E		I		D		D
T	H		X		E		N		C		V		E		A
E	O		T		D		A		U		I		S		I
	L		R				N		M		D		C		N
¹³B	Y		A				I		B				E		I
L		¹⁴P	V				M		E		¹⁵K		N		N
¹⁶I	¹⁷N	E	X	O	R	A	B	¹⁸L	E		I		N		I	S	G
T	S	R		G		O		I		T		I		N		I
H	S	T		A		I		Y		¹⁹O	D	I	O	U	S
E	E	L		N		T				R		N			
	N	Y		C		E		²⁰M	O	R	O	S	E		
	C			E		R				D					
²¹F	E	I	G	N											

Across
1. Protested
5. Enormously; hugely
8. Softens in attitude or temper
10. Poor; penniless
16. Relentless; unyielding
19. Hateful
20. Ill-humored; sullen
21. Pretend

Down
1. Determined
2. Sadness; depression; gloom
3. Filthy; vile
4. Stirred up; disturbed
6. Being courteous with a superior air
7. Treating with scorn or contempt
8. Reclining; lying down
9. Angry; furious
11. Extremely abundant; excessive
12. Complete agreement
13. Joyous; happy
14. Stout; fat
15. Related; belonging to the same family
17. Spirit
18. Hang around; linger

1. ONOIENSNDCECS = 1. _____

    Being courteous with a superior air

2. NMAFOUIS = 2. _____

    Well-known for bad reasons

3. DNTSEICERE = 3. _____

    Pleads on another's behalf

4. TREEBMNCU = 4. _____

    Reclining; lying down

5. TINTOAAERL = 5. _____

    Change

6. UITLULOIRSS = 6. _____

    Glorious; brilliant

7. LXANEIROBE = 7. _____

    Relentless; unyielding

8. NLMCLAHYOE = 8. _____

    Sadness; depression; gloom

9. ETETDRFE = 9. _____

    Shackled; chained

10. RUBESCO = 10. _____

    Dark; vague; unclear

11. TAENLT = 11. _____

    Dormant; hidden

12. CESEESN = 12. _____

    Spirit

13. MOECPSNREDE = 13. _____

    Repaid

14. OCLNENVEBEE = 14. _____

    Generosity; kindness

15. TSUCFIAEO = 15. _____

    Humorous; merry

1. ONOIENSNDCECS
= 1. CONDESCENSION
Being courteous with a superior air

2. NMAFOUIS
= 2. INFAMOUS
Well-known for bad reasons

3. DNTSEICERE
= 3. INTERCEDES
Pleads on another's behalf

4. TREEBMNCU
= 4. RECUMBENT
Reclining; lying down

5. TINTOAAERL
= 5. ALTERATION
Change

6. UITLULOIRSS
= 6. ILLUSTRIOUS
Glorious; brilliant

7. LXANEIROBE
= 7. INEXORABLE
Relentless; unyielding

8. NLMCLAHYOE
= 8. MELANCHOLY
Sadness; depression; gloom

9. ETETDRFE
= 9. FETTERED
Shackled; chained

10. RUBESCO
=10. OBSCURE
Dark; vague; unclear

11. TAENLT
=11. LATENT
Dormant; hidden

12. CESEESN
=12. ESSENCE
Spirit

13. MOECPSNREDE
=13. RECOMPENSED
Repaid

14. OCLNENVEBEE
=14. BENEVOLENCE
Generosity; kindness

15. TSUCFIAEO
=15. FACETIOUS
Humorous; merry

1. ESTPRECP   = 1. _____
Practical rules guiding conduct

2. TCIULSEBPSE   = 2. _____
Impressionable; easily influenced

3. OREMSO   = 3. _____
Ill-humored; sullen

4. ALTNET   = 4. _____
Dormant; hidden

5. IVIDL   = 5. _____
Angry; furious

6. ETRESLN   = 6. _____
Softens in attitude or temper

7. ITTDESUTE   = 7. _____
Poor; penniless

8. EARLBNIOEX   = 8. _____
Relentless; unyielding

9. REBECEALX   = 9. _____
Very bad; offensive

10. NCSAIBNEET   =10. _____
Avoidance

11. ADOTTRENREMS   =11. _____
Protested

12. IINNDGDASI   =12. _____
Treating with scorn or contempt

13. YARRASEVD   =13. _____
Opponent; enemy

14. ETATDISNETO   =14. _____
Intense dislike

15. OSIFMANU   =15. _____
Well-known for bad reasons

1. ESTPRECP   = 1. PRECEPTS
Practical rules guiding conduct

2. TCIULSEBPSE   = 2. SUSCEPTIBLE
Impressionable; easily influenced

3. OREMSO   = 3. MOROSE
Ill-humored; sullen

4. ALTNET   = 4. LATENT
Dormant; hidden

5. IVIDL   = 5. LIVID
Angry; furious

6. ETRESLN   = 6. RELENTS
Softens in attitude or temper

7. ITTDESUTE   = 7. DESTITUTE
Poor; penniless

8. EARLBNIOEX   = 8. INEXORABLE
Relentless; unyielding

9. REBECEALX   = 9. EXECRABLE
Very bad; offensive

10. NCSAIBNEET   =10. ABSTINENCE
Avoidance

11. ADOTTRENREMS   =11. REMONSTRATED
Protested

12. IINNDGDASI   =12. DISDAINING
Treating with scorn or contempt

13. YARRASEVD   =13. ADVERSARY
Opponent; enemy

14. ETATDISNETO   =14. DETESTATION
Intense dislike

15. OSIFMANU   =15. INFAMOUS
Well-known for bad reasons

1. IUODSO   = 1. _____
                              Hateful

2. IANLIUOPTSPC   = 2. _____
                              Asking for humbly or earnestly

3. ENAIARTTLO   = 3. _____
                              Change

4. SCAEIENNTB   = 4. _____
                              Avoidance

5. OICTANOONLS   = 5. _____
                              Comfort; compassion

6. TELESUOR   = 6. _____
                              Determined

7. RSMOOE   = 7. _____
                              Ill-humored; sullen

8. GEAITATD   = 8. _____
                              Stirred up; disturbed

9. IILDV   = 9. _____
                              Angry; furious

10. LROGYODIPSIU   =10. _____
                              Enormously; hugely

11. OCPSSNMAE   =11. _____
                              Surround

12. ALTNET   =12. _____
                              Dormant; hidden

13. TIMINYNAU   =13. _____
                              Complete agreement

14. ORLCYLDIA   =14. _____
                              Graciously; in a friendly way

15. BLHTEI   =15. _____
                              Joyous; happy

1. IUODSO

= 1. ODIOUS

   Hateful

2. IANLIUOPTSPC

= 2. SUPPLICATION

   Asking for humbly or earnestly

3. ENAIARTTLO

= 3. ALTERATION

   Change

4. SCAEIENNTB

= 4. ABSTINENCE

   Avoidance

5. OICTANOONLS

= 5. CONSOLATION

   Comfort; compassion

6. TELESUOR

= 6. RESOLUTE

   Determined

7. RSMOOE

= 7. MOROSE

   Ill-humored; sullen

8. GEAITATD

= 8. AGITATED

   Stirred up; disturbed

9. IILDV

= 9. LIVID

   Angry; furious

10. LROGYODIPSIU

=10. PRODIGIOUSLY

   Enormously; hugely

11. OCPSSNMAE

=11. ENCOMPASS

   Surround

12. ALTNET

=12. LATENT

   Dormant; hidden

13. TIMINYNAU

=13. UNANIMITY

   Complete agreement

14. ORLCYLDIA

=14. CORDIALLY

   Graciously; in a friendly way

15. BLHTEI

=15. BLITHE

   Joyous; happy

1. CSPSAENOM   = 1. _____
   Surround

2. INSTEEAOTDT   = 2. _____
   Intense dislike

3. LNMACLOHYE   = 3. _____
   Sadness; depression; gloom

4. PIULCSEBTES   = 4. _____
   Impressionable; easily influenced

5. THEIBL   = 5. _____
   Joyous; happy

6. ECMTUERBN   = 6. _____
   Reclining; lying down

7. NDGIIAIDNS   = 7. _____
   Treating with scorn or contempt

8. OSMORE   = 8. _____
   Ill-humored; sullen

9. DETEFRTE   = 9. _____
   Shackled; chained

10. IINTYUMNA   =10. _____
   Complete agreement

11. CTESNDERIE   =11. _____
   Pleads on another's behalf

12. IATNRPESDE   =12. _____
   Going on foot; walking

13. OSIUITUBQU   =13. _____
   Being everywhere

14. ROTPLY   =14. _____
   Stout; fat

15. INFGE   =15. _____
   Pretend

1. CSPSAENOM = 1. ENCOMPASS
   Surround

2. INSTEEAOTDT = 2. DETESTATION
   Intense dislike

3. LNMACLOHYE = 3. MELANCHOLY
   Sadness; depression; gloom

4. PIULCSEBTES = 4. SUSCEPTIBLE
   Impressionable; easily influenced

5. THEIBL = 5. BLITHE
   Joyous; happy

6. ECMTUERBN = 6. RECUMBENT
   Reclining; lying down

7. NDGIIAIDNS = 7. DISDAINING
   Treating with scorn or contempt

8. OSMORE = 8. MOROSE
   Ill-humored; sullen

9. DETEFRTE = 9. FETTERED
   Shackled; chained

10. IINTYUMNA =10. UNANIMITY
    Complete agreement

11. CTESNDERIE =11. INTERCEDES
    Pleads on another's behalf

12. IATNRPESDE =12. PEDESTRIAN
    Going on foot; walking

13. OSIUITUBQU =13. UBIQUITOUS
    Being everywhere

14. ROTPLY =14. PORTLY
    Stout; fat

15. INFGE =15. FEIGN
    Pretend

ABSTINENCE	Avoidance
ADVERSARY	Opponent; enemy
AGITATED	Stirred up; disturbed
ALTERATION	Change
BENEVOLENCE	Generosity; kindness
BLITHE	Joyous; happy

CAPACIOUS	Spacious; large
CONDESCENSION	Being courteous with a superior air
CONSOLATION	Comfort; compassion
CORDIALLY	Graciously; in a friendly way
COVETOUS	Desirous of what someone else has
DESTITUTE	Poor; penniless

DETESTATION	Intense dislike
DISDAINING	Treating with scorn or contempt
DISPELLED	Scattered; caused to vanish
ENCOMPASS	Surround
ESSENCE	Spirit
EXECRABLE	Very bad; offensive

EXTRAVAGANCE	Extremely abundant; excessive
FACETIOUS	Humorous; merry
FEIGN	Pretend
FETTERED	Shackled; chained
ILLUSTRIOUS	Glorious; brilliant
INEXORABLE	Relentless; unyielding

INFAMOUS	Well-known for bad reasons
INTERCEDES	Pleads on another's behalf
KINDRED	Related; belonging to the same family
LATENT	Dormant; hidden
LIVID	Angry; furious
LOITER	Hang around; linger

MELANCHOLY	Sadness; depression; gloom
MOROSE	Ill-humored; sullen
OBSCURE	Dark; vague; unclear
ODIOUS	Hateful
OFFICIOUS	Meddlesome; self-important
OMINOUS	Threatening

PEDESTRIAN	Going on foot; walking
PORTLY	Stout; fat
PRECEPTS	Practical rules guiding conduct
PRODIGIOUSLY	Enormously; hugely
RECOMPENSED	Repaid
RECUMBENT	Reclining; lying down

RELENTS	Softens in attitude or temper
REMONSTRATED	Protested
RESOLUTE	Determined
SORDID	Filthy; vile
SUPPLICATION	Asking for humbly or earnestly
SUSCEPTIBLE	Impressionable; easily influenced

UBIQUITOUS	Being everywhere
UNANIMITY	Complete agreement

A Christmas Carol Vocabulary

MELANCHOLY	CAPACIOUS	INTERCEDES	DISDAINING	LATENT
OMINOUS	EXECRABLE	SORDID	LOITER	FETTERED
ESSENCE	LIVID	FREE SPACE	COVETOUS	DETESTATION
INFAMOUS	FEIGN	CONSOLATION	UNANIMITY	OBSCURE
INEXORABLE	ADVERSARY	ENCOMPASS	KINDRED	FACETIOUS

A Christmas Carol Vocabulary

PRODIGIOUSLY	RESOLUTE	ABSTINENCE	MOROSE	CONDESCENSION
PORTLY	RECUMBENT	OFFICIOUS	SUSCEPTIBLE	EXTRAVAGANCE
AGITATED	PEDESTRIAN	FREE SPACE	ALTERATION	CORDIALLY
RECOMPENSED	BLITHE	BENEVOLENCE	RELENTS	DISPELLED
SUPPLICATION	ILLUSTRIOUS	REMONSTRATED	PRECEPTS	ODIOUS

A Christmas Carol Vocabulary

ALTERATION	OBSCURE	INFAMOUS	PRODIGIOUSLY	SUSCEPTIBLE
LIVID	FEIGN	ABSTINENCE	CONDESCENSION	FACETIOUS
DISPELLED	COVETOUS	FREE SPACE	OFFICIOUS	ADVERSARY
CAPACIOUS	ENCOMPASS	UBIQUITOUS	DISDAINING	PEDESTRIAN
CONSOLATION	MELANCHOLY	OMINOUS	DETESTATION	INEXORABLE

A Christmas Carol Vocabulary

SUPPLICATION	RECOMPENSED	FETTERED	RECUMBENT	ESSENCE
REMONSTRATED	EXECRABLE	UNANIMITY	PRECEPTS	CORDIALLY
KINDRED	EXTRAVAGANCE	FREE SPACE	AGITATED	ODIOUS
RELENTS	RESOLUTE	INTERCEDES	PORTLY	SORDID
BLITHE	LATENT	BENEVOLENCE	MOROSE	LOITER

A Christmas Carol Vocabulary

ENCOMPASS	MELANCHOLY	FACETIOUS	DISDAINING	LIVID
LATENT	RESOLUTE	MOROSE	ILLUSTRIOUS	OBSCURE
BLITHE	AGITATED	FREE SPACE	SUPPLICATION	EXECRABLE
BENEVOLENCE	LOITER	RELENTS	PORTLY	DESTITUTE
INEXORABLE	FEIGN	RECOMPENSED	DETESTATION	CONSOLATION

A Christmas Carol Vocabulary

PEDESTRIAN	OMINOUS	DISPELLED	SUSCEPTIBLE	CONDESCENSION
ADVERSARY	COVETOUS	PRODIGIOUSLY	CORDIALLY	UBIQUITOUS
CAPACIOUS	INFAMOUS	FREE SPACE	ALTERATION	REMONSTRATED
INTERCEDES	ABSTINENCE	EXTRAVAGANCE	FETTERED	SORDID
ODIOUS	RECUMBENT	KINDRED	ESSENCE	UNANIMITY

A Christmas Carol Vocabulary

OFFICIOUS	RESOLUTE	OBSCURE	KINDRED	PEDESTRIAN
BLITHE	DETESTATION	BENEVOLENCE	CONSOLATION	PRODIGIOUSLY
DISDAINING	CAPACIOUS	FREE SPACE	RECUMBENT	ABSTINENCE
INTERCEDES	OMINOUS	MOROSE	COVETOUS	LIVID
FETTERED	FACETIOUS	RECOMPENSED	EXECRABLE	LOITER

A Christmas Carol Vocabulary

CONDESCENSION	INEXORABLE	PORTLY	SORDID	ODIOUS
INFAMOUS	UNANIMITY	LATENT	FEIGN	SUPPLICATION
ESSENCE	AGITATED	FREE SPACE	RELENTS	DISPELLED
REMONSTRATED	SUSCEPTIBLE	ALTERATION	MELANCHOLY	ILLUSTRIOUS
ADVERSARY	EXTRAVAGANCE	CORDIALLY	DESTITUTE	PRECEPTS

A Christmas Carol Vocabulary

ILLUSTRIOUS	INTERCEDES	LOITER	DESTITUTE	SUPPLICATION
ESSENCE	OMINOUS	MOROSE	SUSCEPTIBLE	LIVID
UNANIMITY	BLITHE	FREE SPACE	KINDRED	FACETIOUS
RECOMPENSED	SORDID	ABSTINENCE	CAPACIOUS	PRODIGIOUSLY
ADVERSARY	INEXORABLE	LATENT	INFAMOUS	ENCOMPASS

A Christmas Carol Vocabulary

REMONSTRATED	OFFICIOUS	RESOLUTE	FEIGN	AGITATED
ALTERATION	FETTERED	EXTRAVAGANCE	CONDESCENSION	DISPELLED
PORTLY	CORDIALLY	FREE SPACE	EXECRABLE	OBSCURE
COVETOUS	DETESTATION	MELANCHOLY	RELENTS	ODIOUS
UBIQUITOUS	BENEVOLENCE	PRECEPTS	RECUMBENT	DISDAINING

A Christmas Carol Vocabulary

FETTERED	PEDESTRIAN	RECUMBENT	UBIQUITOUS	CORDIALLY
AGITATED	OFFICIOUS	INTERCEDES	CAPACIOUS	OBSCURE
REMONSTRATED	DISPELLED	FREE SPACE	PORTLY	SORDID
COVETOUS	LIVID	UNANIMITY	RESOLUTE	INEXORABLE
ESSENCE	DISDAINING	OMINOUS	FACETIOUS	DESTITUTE

A Christmas Carol Vocabulary

DETESTATION	CONDESCENSION	CONSOLATION	INFAMOUS	ABSTINENCE
FEIGN	ODIOUS	BENEVOLENCE	ENCOMPASS	BLITHE
LOITER	LATENT	FREE SPACE	EXECRABLE	PRECEPTS
MELANCHOLY	ADVERSARY	ILLUSTRIOUS	RECOMPENSED	MOROSE
KINDRED	ALTERATION	SUSCEPTIBLE	SUPPLICATION	EXTRAVAGANCE

A Christmas Carol Vocabulary

COVETOUS	OMINOUS	INEXORABLE	PRECEPTS	ENCOMPASS
PORTLY	BLITHE	UBIQUITOUS	CONSOLATION	DETESTATION
PRODIGIOUSLY	ODIOUS	FREE SPACE	ADVERSARY	FACETIOUS
INTERCEDES	KINDRED	INFAMOUS	PEDESTRIAN	UNANIMITY
BENEVOLENCE	CORDIALLY	SORDID	DISPELLED	ILLUSTRIOUS

A Christmas Carol Vocabulary

CAPACIOUS	RECUMBENT	ABSTINENCE	EXTRAVAGANCE	RECOMPENSED
EXECRABLE	RESOLUTE	LOITER	CONDESCENSION	ESSENCE
MELANCHOLY	LIVID	FREE SPACE	LATENT	SUPPLICATION
AGITATED	RELENTS	ALTERATION	MOROSE	SUSCEPTIBLE
DISDAINING	DESTITUTE	OBSCURE	OFFICIOUS	FEIGN

A Christmas Carol Vocabulary

OBSCURE	UNANIMITY	RELENTS	PRECEPTS	INTERCEDES
EXTRAVAGANCE	PEDESTRIAN	FACETIOUS	CAPACIOUS	DETESTATION
DISDAINING	BLITHE	FREE SPACE	CONDESCENSION	MOROSE
FEIGN	INEXORABLE	OFFICIOUS	MELANCHOLY	BENEVOLENCE
RECOMPENSED	RECUMBENT	ABSTINENCE	DESTITUTE	PRODIGIOUSLY

A Christmas Carol Vocabulary

REMONSTRATED	EXECRABLE	ALTERATION	FETTERED	PORTLY
LATENT	OMINOUS	LOITER	SUSCEPTIBLE	ODIOUS
ESSENCE	CONSOLATION	FREE SPACE	UBIQUITOUS	ENCOMPASS
INFAMOUS	KINDRED	ILLUSTRIOUS	SUPPLICATION	SORDID
DISPELLED	COVETOUS	RESOLUTE	ADVERSARY	AGITATED

A Christmas Carol Vocabulary

OFFICIOUS	FEIGN	RELENTS	FACETIOUS	AGITATED
EXTRAVAGANCE	DISPELLED	LIVID	LATENT	CORDIALLY
CAPACIOUS	INFAMOUS	FREE SPACE	ESSENCE	INEXORABLE
DISDAINING	FETTERED	BLITHE	UBIQUITOUS	SUSCEPTIBLE
SORDID	PRODIGIOUSLY	MOROSE	DESTITUTE	RESOLUTE

A Christmas Carol Vocabulary

DETESTATION	ADVERSARY	CONDESCENSION	PORTLY	LOITER
BENEVOLENCE	ABSTINENCE	ALTERATION	INTERCEDES	EXECRABLE
CONSOLATION	KINDRED	FREE SPACE	ODIOUS	RECUMBENT
REMONSTRATED	PEDESTRIAN	OMINOUS	UNANIMITY	ENCOMPASS
RECOMPENSED	MELANCHOLY	SUPPLICATION	PRECEPTS	ILLUSTRIOUS

A Christmas Carol Vocabulary

ESSENCE	CAPACIOUS	RECOMPENSED	DETESTATION	MOROSE
PRECEPTS	SORDID	CORDIALLY	FETTERED	ILLUSTRIOUS
SUSCEPTIBLE	PRODIGIOUSLY	FREE SPACE	DISDAINING	ODIOUS
REMONSTRATED	ALTERATION	COVETOUS	INTERCEDES	EXECRABLE
PEDESTRIAN	ABSTINENCE	SUPPLICATION	INFAMOUS	BLITHE

A Christmas Carol Vocabulary

LOITER	RESOLUTE	ENCOMPASS	KINDRED	UBIQUITOUS
INEXORABLE	CONSOLATION	OBSCURE	ADVERSARY	BENEVOLENCE
EXTRAVAGANCE	MELANCHOLY	FREE SPACE	PORTLY	UNANIMITY
RELENTS	LATENT	FEIGN	FACETIOUS	OMINOUS
AGITATED	LIVID	OFFICIOUS	DISPELLED	RECUMBENT

A Christmas Carol Vocabulary

KINDRED	ODIOUS	DISDAINING	DETESTATION	ENCOMPASS
UBIQUITOUS	OFFICIOUS	LOITER	OBSCURE	SUSCEPTIBLE
DISPELLED	AGITATED	FREE SPACE	CONDESCENSION	DESTITUTE
FETTERED	INFAMOUS	BLITHE	EXTRAVAGANCE	BENEVOLENCE
SUPPLICATION	ADVERSARY	CONSOLATION	PRODIGIOUSLY	PRECEPTS

A Christmas Carol Vocabulary

ABSTINENCE	UNANIMITY	ALTERATION	RECOMPENSED	MOROSE
CORDIALLY	ILLUSTRIOUS	FACETIOUS	REMONSTRATED	PORTLY
INTERCEDES	FEIGN	FREE SPACE	INEXORABLE	RECUMBENT
PEDESTRIAN	COVETOUS	LATENT	RELENTS	LIVID
EXECRABLE	SORDID	RESOLUTE	ESSENCE	MELANCHOLY

A Christmas Carol Vocabulary

ESSENCE	DISDAINING	FACETIOUS	RECOMPENSED	LIVID
LOITER	INTERCEDES	INEXORABLE	PORTLY	KINDRED
SORDID	MOROSE	FREE SPACE	RECUMBENT	INFAMOUS
RESOLUTE	BLITHE	CONDESCENSION	PRODIGIOUSLY	ILLUSTRIOUS
PRECEPTS	CORDIALLY	ABSTINENCE	PEDESTRIAN	SUPPLICATION

A Christmas Carol Vocabulary

OBSCURE	ADVERSARY	EXTRAVAGANCE	OMINOUS	CONSOLATION
DISPELLED	UBIQUITOUS	LATENT	FEIGN	DETESTATION
BENEVOLENCE	ENCOMPASS	FREE SPACE	RELENTS	UNANIMITY
DESTITUTE	SUSCEPTIBLE	CAPACIOUS	OFFICIOUS	AGITATED
COVETOUS	EXECRABLE	REMONSTRATED	MELANCHOLY	ODIOUS

A Christmas Carol Vocabulary

SUPPLICATION	PRODIGIOUSLY	PRECEPTS	INTERCEDES	COVETOUS
DISDAINING	DESTITUTE	UNANIMITY	MELANCHOLY	LATENT
UBIQUITOUS	PEDESTRIAN	FREE SPACE	REMONSTRATED	FETTERED
BENEVOLENCE	RECOMPENSED	PORTLY	AGITATED	OMINOUS
CORDIALLY	CONDESCENSION	DISPELLED	ADVERSARY	LIVID

A Christmas Carol Vocabulary

LOITER	SUSCEPTIBLE	ODIOUS	SORDID	INEXORABLE
BLITHE	FEIGN	EXTRAVAGANCE	ALTERATION	CAPACIOUS
OBSCURE	CONSOLATION	FREE SPACE	OFFICIOUS	ABSTINENCE
RELENTS	RECUMBENT	ESSENCE	RESOLUTE	FACETIOUS
KINDRED	INFAMOUS	EXECRABLE	MOROSE	ENCOMPASS

A Christmas Carol Vocabulary

UNANIMITY	CONDESCENSION	ABSTINENCE	INFAMOUS	ENCOMPASS
MOROSE	ILLUSTRIOUS	DISPELLED	CORDIALLY	INEXORABLE
COVETOUS	INTERCEDES	FREE SPACE	SORDID	FETTERED
PORTLY	PEDESTRIAN	ESSENCE	FACETIOUS	RECOMPENSED
DETESTATION	ODIOUS	BLITHE	OBSCURE	PRECEPTS

A Christmas Carol Vocabulary

PRODIGIOUSLY	UBIQUITOUS	BENEVOLENCE	CONSOLATION	KINDRED
OFFICIOUS	EXECRABLE	AGITATED	SUSCEPTIBLE	RELENTS
ALTERATION	MELANCHOLY	FREE SPACE	CAPACIOUS	DESTITUTE
RESOLUTE	SUPPLICATION	OMINOUS	DISDAINING	LOITER
ADVERSARY	EXTRAVAGANCE	RECUMBENT	LATENT	REMONSTRATED

A Christmas Carol Vocabulary

UBIQUITOUS	ALTERATION	PEDESTRIAN	ODIOUS	PRODIGIOUSLY
ABSTINENCE	EXTRAVAGANCE	SUPPLICATION	CONSOLATION	CORDIALLY
SUSCEPTIBLE	UNANIMITY	FREE SPACE	MOROSE	FEIGN
OBSCURE	CAPACIOUS	ADVERSARY	AGITATED	BLITHE
ESSENCE	INEXORABLE	SORDID	EXECRABLE	DISDAINING

A Christmas Carol Vocabulary

DETESTATION	PRECEPTS	REMONSTRATED	RECUMBENT	DESTITUTE
OMINOUS	RESOLUTE	BENEVOLENCE	PORTLY	INFAMOUS
FETTERED	DISPELLED	FREE SPACE	RECOMPENSED	ILLUSTRIOUS
RELENTS	LIVID	OFFICIOUS	INTERCEDES	COVETOUS
LATENT	ENCOMPASS	CONDESCENSION	KINDRED	FACETIOUS

A Christmas Carol Vocabulary

PRODIGIOUSLY	CONDESCENSION	LATENT	INEXORABLE	CAPACIOUS
DISPELLED	OBSCURE	LIVID	PORTLY	ABSTINENCE
BLITHE	SUSCEPTIBLE	FREE SPACE	CORDIALLY	INTERCEDES
AGITATED	RECOMPENSED	REMONSTRATED	MOROSE	BENEVOLENCE
ESSENCE	LOITER	RECUMBENT	MELANCHOLY	COVETOUS

A Christmas Carol Vocabulary

INFAMOUS	ILLUSTRIOUS	ALTERATION	FACETIOUS	SORDID
DESTITUTE	DISDAINING	RELENTS	OMINOUS	PRECEPTS
EXECRABLE	UBIQUITOUS	FREE SPACE	FETTERED	KINDRED
FEIGN	PEDESTRIAN	OFFICIOUS	UNANIMITY	DETESTATION
RESOLUTE	EXTRAVAGANCE	ADVERSARY	CONSOLATION	ENCOMPASS